Dance
Like You Mean It

by Jim Banks

www.jimandpatbanks.com
www.traumaprayer.com

email: jim.banks55@gmail.com

1st Printing 2020

All scripture quotations, unless otherwise noted, are taken from the Holy Bible, Authorized King James Version, Public Domain, or from the Revised Standard Version of the Bible, copyright 1952 [2nd edition, 1971] by the Division of Christian Education of the National Council of the Churches of Christ in the United States of America. Scripture quotations marked (NKJV) are taken from the New King James Version. Copyright 1982, Thomas Nelson, used by permission.

Quotations marked (ESV) are taken from The Holy Bible, English Standard Version. ESV® Permanent Text Edition ® (2016). Copyright © 2001 by Crossway Bibles, a publishing ministry of Good News Publishers. All Rights Reserved.

Please note that Jim's publishing style capitalizes certain pronouns in Scripture that refer to the Father, Son, and Holy Spirit and may differ from some Bible publishers' style.

Please note that the name satan and any related names are purposely not capitalized. We choose not to acknowledge him even to the point of violating grammatical rules.

Copyright © Jim Banks
All Rights Reserved. No part of this book may be reproduced in any form, except for the inclusions of brief quotations in review, without expressed written permission by the author/publisher.

Other books by Jim Banks;

The Effects of Trauma and How to Deal With It, 3rd Edition
A Workbook to accompany the above book
Finding Your Life Calling
The Insidious Dance, The Paralysis of Perfectionism
Defeating Jezebel
One Calling, One Ministry, A Couple's Guide to Finding Your Calling
Helping Your Veteran Deal With The Effects of Trauma (PTSD)
Boundaries
Hope for Freedom
Angels and Demons
Sex Trafficking Ministry Manual w/ Becca Wineka
Cast A Long Shadow
Finishing Well
Choose Your Outcome w/ Mandy Valdes
The Enemy Within
Just Thinking
Land Cleansing 101. Your birthright & your responsibility

All these books are available through Amaxon.com

About the Author

I, Jim Banks, was born immediately following WWII in Mexia, Texas, which is about 45 miles east of Waco, TX. Although at the time of this writing, in spite of the fact that I am currently a residing in the Nashville, TN area, I still feel significant drawings to the Republic of Texas. My dad went to college at Baylor, my mom at Texas Tech, both my brother and sister went to Texas A&M. Both sets of my grandparents lived, died and are buried there. It's true, you can take the boy out of Texas, but you can't take Texas out of the boy.

I was raised all over the Southern and Western halves of the US, and either lived or worked in all but five States in the Union, and consequently don't have that characteristic Texas drawl to my voice, as many of you may have noticed by listening to the audio version of the Trauma Prayer available from our web sites, www.jimandpatbanks.com or, www.traumaprayer.com, or from various postings on YouTube. So I still occasionally wear my "manly footwear" as Gary P. Nunn sang about in "London Homesick Blues" and I have also been known to periodically don the appropriate head wear.

I graduated from Covington High School in Covington, LA, entered the Air Force in '66 and finished college at The University of Southwest Louisiana in Lafayette, LA in Electrical Engineering. I went to work for a consulting engineering firm in Houston, TX in 1974 as a designer of power systems. That's when I discovered that engineering and my perfectionist tendencies were not an easy, freewheeling, harmonious match. Three and a half years later I left engineering for a career in industrial sales and marketing for a series of controls equipment manufacturers where I became Director of Sales & Marketing for a couple of those companies.

I was fortunate enough to marry the former Patricia Smith in Houston in July of 1980 and we immediately left "all our exes in Texas" and moved to Indianapolis, IN. My technical sales employment took us to Colorado where we experienced an "in-over-our-heads" plunge into personal ministry activity and an introduction into the mysteries of the operation of the Holy Spirit when we began working part for a Christian ministry in Windsor, CO.

However, our initial introduction to ministry came as a result of working with a group of young married couples in a Southern Baptist church in Indianapolis shortly after we were married. The experience of seeing individuals fall, helping to pick them up, dust them off, apply a bandage or two then sending them back out again, only to see the same thing happen again in a few weeks or months brought us to the realization that there was something missing and there was a lot we didn't know, but needed desperately.

In our zeal to help people we made the rookie mistake of uttering this infamous prayer, "If you will teach us how to heal broken hearts and broken people we'll give our lives to it." We somehow had in our naive little minds that we'd go to a three or four day seminar somewhere and Bingo! we'd have everything we needed to change our little world. The fact that our rude introduction was complicated slightly by the presence of demons caused us to have to look outside our Southern Baptist resource circle, which at the time seemed to be totally devoid of understanding about this arena.

Obviously, this is when our real education began; reading everything we could get our hands on forced us to become life-long learners.

The more you think you know only seems to reveal how little you actually know.

The initiation into the answer to that earlier prayer began in earnest when we moved to Loveland, Colorado a couple of years later and we joined the ministry of Derin Carmack, (now deceased) first as part-time phone ministers, then as personal assistant (Jim) and business manager (Pat).

Coincident with a major industrial market implosion due to the recession of the late 80's we sold our home and moved from Loveland, Colorado to the Atlanta area. Sandwiched in between was a 9 month stint back in Covington, LA to attend my father as he died of cancer, which is another story in itself.

The move to Atlanta took me back into electrical design engineering again, and brought a bit more structure to our personal ministry activity, which we did nights and weekends out of our home. At this point the ministry often became a ministry arm of the local churches we were members of. Sometimes this was good … other times, not so much. People and the workings of the institutional church are strange bedfellows.

In 2002 we moved from the Atlanta area to Asheville, NC, which opened the door for us to move into ministry on a full-time basis. While in Asheville in 2004, we founded a healing room, which within a few months offered a comprehensive healing regimen, through numerous tools and programs, to the entire region.

I used the term 'comprehensive' purposefully for regardless of a client's presenting issue we offered something for everyone at some point in time throughout the week. Members of that volunteer group, which at one point in time was almost 50 people from 5 different churches, met at various times during the week at a church in an eastern suburb of Asheville, and as far as I know it is still operating as of this publishing. During this period we had a permanent office location which opened the door for us to see numerous clients for personal ministry each week in a permanent location.

It was during this season that land cleansing became a big "thing" for me. Asheville, like so many other locations in our nation, had become sacred ground for so many people groups and religions throughout history, which made it a very 'spiritual' place. Unfortunately, all the mainline denominations established their retreat centers in the mountains around Asheville and in so doing, abandoned the valley to the devil, evoking the memory of 1King 20:23 when the Syrians said that,

> *"Their gods are gods of the hills; therefore they were stronger than we; but let us fight against them in the plain, and surely we shall be stronger than they."*

I believe that one of the major keys to our ministry success has been a commitment to go somewhere new for personal ministry every year to 18 months. This has introduced us to many new ministry techniques, tools and philosophies over the years, and has done wonders to broaden the effectiveness of our ministry and our marriage.

In 2008 I discovered the basic constituent pieces of what has become known as the Trauma Prayer, available from our web sites, www.jimandpatbanks.com or www.traumaprayer.com, or from various postings on YouTube. This 23 minute recording has been downloaded, viewed and copied for distribution by over 2,500,000 people around the world, which has opened the doors for personal ministry and training significantly. About 40,000 people got to sleep to it every night.

My wife and I currently live in Nashville, TN area and are struggling to become rabid Titans fans. Although we are major sports fans, we've never been huge college sports fans after saying goodbye to the old SW Conference football excitement to move to Indiana.

You have to understand, we were living in Indianapolis when the owner of the Baltimore Colts moved them to Indy surreptitiously in the middle of the night. Then we lived in Colorado during the days of John Elway and the Orange Crush. If you were not passionate about the Broncos in those days you would be forced to leave the State. Following Colorado we suffered through a period in south Louisiana when the New Orleans Saints were the "aints", and then on to Atlanta when Jerry Glanville was leaving tickets for Elvis at the Will-Call box for Falcons football games, and future Hall-of-Famer, John Smoltz was giving up more first inning runs for the Braves than a pair of cheap nylon stockings.

These days I am still a sailor wanna-be after selling all our boats, I sailed in high school as a foredeck monkey on some 30 and 40 footers, and sailed competitively all through college. I am a solid bogey golfer and an avid fly fisherman. These days that's about the limit of my sports enthusiasm, although we do try to catch an NFL game on TV when we are not traveling. In the last few years we seemed to have been either in Africa or in Asia through half the season, so even our ardor for professional football has waned – helped along by the whole kneeling during the national anthem business.

We are the proud parents of two girls and two boys, and to date have six grandchildren, all of whom live east of the Mississippi.

Pat enjoys bossing me around, while I still enjoy trout fishing, sailing and golf, although I don't get to participate in them as much as I'd like to become accustomed. If you would like to offer help in these departments I'm sure you would find me a willing and grateful companion.

Blessings, Jim Banks.

1

Introduction

This book is about "walking in the spirit." Actually it might be more accurate to say "stumbling" in the spirit, since it seems we are a whole lot better at that than actually walking or running with any level of confidence. I am not sure who coined that phrase originally, nor why he or she didn't use the word "ambling." I certainly understand why they shied away from using the word "running."

Nonetheless, in some respects this work is an attempt to fit into the category of a "How To" book, but that would presume it to cover a whole lot more ground than I am going to attempt. I have learned a few things about living and stumbling in the spirit in the last 40 years of trying to follow the Lord, yet I have a long way to go before I could be considered any kind of an expert on the topic.

What I want to convey are some of the more practical things the Lord has ushered me into that most of the people I work with are somehow not privy to. For many it's the religious traditions they have chosen to remain focused on as though they felt they had to reach some level of maturity before they could enter into the practical application of it. I suppose this is due to our Western viewpoint that I have to graduate from the class before I can be considered qualified to do such a thing.

For others it doesn't feel safe because of some teaching they've had from people who were also taught that it wasn't safe – you could wind up out in the spiritual weeds somewhere and find yourself being disqualified from even being a normal human again. And then there are those who are satisfied where they are and don't have a hunger for more. However, there is a large population in Christendom that have just never been exposed to the fact that this is the life they were created to walk in; one that is both spiritually exciting and productive for the Kingdom of God.

So my aim is an introduction to your supernatural capabilities by giving you some insight into mine. So, some background is in order.

My wife and I have been heavily involved in the inner healing and deliverance business for over three decades, and full time for the last eighteen years, trying to help people deal with the spiritual, emotional and mental implications of abuse, wounding and trauma. For those of you who are not familiar with it, inner healing is simply the process of resolving the short and long term effects of the wounds, tragedies and traumas, the bumps and bruises, and such, along with the myriad of lies and half-truth that were implanted following those events that was behind the creation of the dysfunctional behaviors, fear and phobias people live with from living life on this messed up planet.

These abrupt interruptions in our otherwise less-than-tranquil lives are the result of our parent's actions or disconnectedness, their abuse or misuse of correction methods, multiple incidents of rejection, physical and relational abandonment, betrayals, untimely deaths and divorces, broken relationships, or any one of a thousand other things.

Essentially, the reason behind all these difficulties (or tribulations, as Jesus called them) is to keep you from walking in the spirit, because you are still limping around in the flesh, seemingly satisfied that this is as good as it gets. One thing that difficulties initiate is that they tend to turn us inward and away from caring about the needs of others, or at least to the extent that we'll fail to do something about them.

A very brief introduction to how we got involved in this business was included the opening Chapter entitled "About the Author." Suffice it to say that our initial exposure to the broken and demonized among those we cared for was sufficient to propel us eventually into full time ministry.

We prayed that prayer simply because we didn't know how to help them and had grown tired of feeling impotent in the face of their struggles.

Essentially, that feeling was one more of the previously noted elements that slows the sanctification process down to a snail's pace. Inner healing is the act of divesting ourselves of the baggage of the wounds and the behavior and beliefs that significantly negative event created that will not allow us, or makes it extremely difficult, to be conformed to the image of Jesus Christ. It is also generally the things that keep us from enjoying life and preventing us from being fulfilled by the work of our hands.

Anyway you cut it life is hard, and harder for some than for others. The cumulative effect of these wounds is the inability to live with an open heart toward others, or the basic trust that is necessary to maintain close life-giving relationships over an extended period of time. When coupled with the dysfunctional coping mechanisms we adopt to help protect ourselves from being hurt or taken advantage of again, life becomes even more difficult and less enjoyable.

The strategy of the enemy is to get you to live totally out of your head, rather than your heart, consequently, "walking in the spirit" is impossible, because you have to figure everything out.

Let me give you an everyday example of the consequences of wounds and a dedication to self-protect that perhaps you have experienced. There is a waitress at one of our local restaurants who is a very beautiful girl physically. She appears to carry herself with much style and grace, and yet when she comes to your table, only her body shows up. The real person is nowhere to be seen because all her walls are up and are seemingly impenetrable. She thinks she's doing a great job, however the customers have a different opinion, even though she does an effective job as a server. They think she's aloof, dispassionate and cares little if they enjoy their dining experience or not. Don't get me wrong, she does care about what she's supposed to do, but her work would carry the description of "perfunctory." Not exactly what her boss, or we as customers, would like to have in a server.

Perfunctory execution of personal responsibilities doesn't engender high praise from anyone, nor does it produce any level of self-satisfaction because she doesn't give her all to it – she just shows up. Were you to ask her about how well she's doing, she could probably point to several 'accomplishments' because she's doing all she knows to do with what she brings to the table.

Some would write this off as just her personality, but you have to understand that she's only warm and outgoing among those she trusts. They reality of the effects of her closed spirit is reflected in how everyone else views her behavior.

Collectively, we are looking for and readily appreciate authenticity, openness, warmth and genuineness in people regardless of what they do, or even how well they do it. If you are present and working hard people will give you multiple chances when you do poorly. In other words, we enjoy it when someone gives their all to what they have at hand. It's a genuine pleasure to be around such people. If I can't engage the real you, my experience is not going to be good, particularly if you are in the service business.

Consequently, living with the effects of all the traumas, wounds and afflictions we accumulate in life and will cause you to not live life authentically and it will prevent you from acting like your true self. In other words, a person's wounded and broken soul is stifling the activity and expression of their human spirit.

In essence, folks like her think they would prefer to be someone else, someone who is more well liked, has more friends, is more popular, is less rejectable, more lovable and consequently, immanently more successful in business and social relationships. To accomplish that they either have to shut some part of themselves down, try to cut it off, or try to be something other than who they are because they think it will provide them with the personal security and protection they need.

The problem is that somewhere along life's journey they will find that they don't really know who they are because they've tried to be somebody else all their lives. Consequently, they can never quite figure out why they're here, or what they are supposed to do with their lives. So they wander aimlessly looking for the place and career that fits them and never seem to find it anywhere … and where they are currently (wherever that is) doesn't seem to fit either. Historically, it's been identified as a "mid-life crisis."

From my vantage point, for many people the pursuit of healing wounds has unfortunately become a life-long objective hoping that when it's finally done they'll know who they are and where they fit, and finally their future will be open and available to them. That maze never has any cheese in it, for there's always one more wound to heal. That will always keep your future out there somewhere waiting for you to get healed.

The message of mainline denominational Christianity has even fostered this viewpoint by harping on being sinless as the way to being holy and thus fulfill the commands of Christ, as though with the appropriate amount of human effort, self-denial, perseverance, dedication and self flagellation we'll arrive at the pinnacle of both God's and human acceptance. Primarily the message is don't do this, don't do that, don't, don't, don't.

If that is what you've been taught, welcome to the ultimate misery.

Confidentially, I don't think I have ever responded well to any list of "Don'ts" no matter who promulgated it, except the one that said, "Don't mess with snakes." I've done really well with that one. Otherwise, the list of "Don'ts" seemed more like an open invitation to indulge because the one fostering it didn't seem like they had ever had any fun in their entire miserable little lives so why should I listen to them? The act of focusing on the negative never created anything positive for me. Isn't that what the Apostle Paul said In Romans 7:5-24; the law (rules and regulations) which were supposed to bring life, only brought death to him.

Because we are human and live in a fallen world, we somehow still believe in the power of rules and the efficacy of focusing on the negative to keep us safe and make us more acceptable to God and man. It's as though we are programmed to live by "if I do right, everything will be right."

We are acutely aware of all of our personal failures, where we could have tried harder, made another choice, done things differently, or should have not done this or that. We have all worked hard at "never doing that again" and repeatedly found ourselves making the same vow over and over again, just in seemingly different circumstances, *"Lord, if you'll get me out of this mess, I swear, I'll never do that again!"*

We've all done it and are very aware of trying to do better … as well as our eventual failure to fulfill our own desires and expectations for improvement.

The bottom line is that there is a much better way to live, one that incidentally is also much less problematic and doesn't require us to first fix all our wounds and correct all of our foibles in order to enter it.

Does that mean that healing wounds and resolving issues is not important and shouldn't be pursued? No, not at all! Todd White, as great a guy as he is, is flat wrong. (I am not so sure his wife would totally agree.) He was miraculously saved and delivered of addiction, and all manner of other crap while high on drugs. So for him to form a concrete theology around his personal experience and declare that you have no need of inner healing or generational deliverance because of Jesus and you are a new creature in Christ, old things have passed away, behold all things have become new, works great for him – so far. Unfortunately, as true as that is for him, one size doesn't fit all. The majority of us have to work out our salvation and if I picked up anything from the Apostle Paul's writing in Romans 6 and 7 is that the flesh dies hard, and the war between flesh and spirit is indeed a struggle.

What I am trying to say is that some degree of introspection is helpful in life, but as a steady diet, it is counterproductive. Introspection at least from the standpoint of focusing on your problems and staying on a continuous internal search for a solution is not helpful. If it goes on long enough you come to identify more with the problem than the healed person that you desire to be. As long as your focus is on fixing the negative, all you're going to see is more negative stuff to fix or heal. So you can never really enter into wholeness because over time you will have fostered the idea that there is something else to be conquered that will allow you to freely walk into your "destiny." The destination is never achieved.

Let me give you an example. Pat and I were ministering to a woman in her late 50's who was always wanting ministry for something or another. She would hear that we had used some tool she'd never heard of on somebody to good affect and she would come running. I asked her one day, 'What would it look like to you if you were to get all your wounds healed?' Her countenance quickly brightened and she sat straight up in the chair and proclaimed that it would means that she could get out of bed in the morning and not hurt. My first thought was, Honey there ain't never gonna be any days like that for you because of your age, the damage you've done to your body, being significantly overweight and out of condition. Fortunately, I was able to convey that truth in a much more consumable manner. When our focus is on the wrong thing, we totally ignore the facts of life, then our motivation for getting there morphs into something unrealistic.

When that is your viewpoint, what do you do with natural resistance, obstacles, oppositions, challenges and struggles to make progress in any area? If your focus is always inward then eventually your deduction from the weight of all the evidence presented is – I am the problem.

The real sorrow of that kind of focus is that your future is always "out there somewhere" waiting for you to get healed, and always presents solid reasons why you I can't enter it until you finally pass through that last gate.

Let me give you another take on introspection. Introspection is not what I would consider mindfulness. Wounding typically causes people to live totally out of their heads, they are not in contact with their own emotions at all. Consequently, they have little or no discernment at all, which is largely communicated via your emotions. So we must learn to live with our emotions actively intact at all times. That is not introspection. That is more about discovering what you think and how you got there. So many of those I minister to have chosen to live in denial because they feel that if they can live without troubling emotions, they can be much happier.

So over the last few years we have come to realize that ministerially we needed to move away from a focus on inner healing because at the core, our ministry is actually the process of helping individuals re-establish, or discover their personal identity, coupled with helping people learn how to walk "spirit-forward." That changes everything.

Often there is some healing that has to be accomplished in order to get there, which is normal, but once identity is realized everything changes; personal vision and purpose replaces the endless search for answers and solutions that allows life to once again become filled with the compelling engagement of solving the world's problems rather than your own. That gives meaning and fulfillment to living, making life rich and satisfying.

It is interesting to think that the Western idea that spawned our universalist "cause and effect" thinking is actually the source of this life-long introspective phenomenon. If I can just find the source of the problem, then I can fix it and all will be well. That's pretty much BS and I believe I can show you just how off base it is.

What I want to do in this book is to walk you through some of the foundation of this insight we've come to, which will include the background of the cosmic war that is being fought all around us that you and we have incidentally become part of; the discovery of why life has been so hard for you specifically; who and what you are up against and how to begin making the transition to that place your heart knew existed all along, but didn't know how to identify or how to enter.

Hang on, because to embrace some of this you will have to stop and digest it for a bit in order to see the truth of it and the value in it. That's a good thing because a great deal of what we have believed to this point has been re-shaped and re-interpreted by the system of the world we live in and not by the One who created it.

It is my prayer that in thinking about what will be presented here, you will see it from a "big picture point of view." The American gospel has become rather narcissistic, in that it is largely about you and I getting saved, and not additionally becoming who you were meant to be (disciples with a specific realm of influence) in the overall scheme of things of the Kingdom. Then religion takes over and makes the principles of the Bible all about an intellectual exercise in mental assent to ideas contained in specific passages, mostly taken out of context.

For those of you who have read any of my other books you will find some pieces of this material in one or more of them. This is the only place (to date) where this complete viewpoint has been assembled and is the whole reason I felt compelled to do it. I hope that you too will find it as valuable to you as those I have taught it to over the years. Those who have chosen to apply it have experienced life changing results.

I leave you with this …

> *"Contentment with earthly goods is the mark of a saint. Contentment with our spiritual state is a mark of inward blindness. Orthodox Christianity has fallen to its present lower state from lack of spiritual desire. Among the*

many who profess the Christian faith, scarcely one in a thousand reveal any passionate thirst for God." A.W. Tozer

2

Dance Like You Mean It

Someday I may come up with a better title than this, but this will have to suffice until I can think of something that is more descriptive of what I am trying to convey. The difficulty for us as Christians is that we know that we are to live in the spirit (dance, if you will) but rather than give our all to it, we get out on the floor and wander around to the music and call it dancing.

Do you remember those early days of Junior High, or your Freshman/Sophomore year in High School, when that first occasion to actually dance with someone of the opposite sex, that wasn't a member of your family loomed heavy on the horizon? The Prom. There was huge nervous excitement about the whole event; getting really dressed up for the first time, a corsage, seeing all your friends there – all dolled up for the evening, perhaps even the thrill of your first real date. When the thought of how to dance crept up, we typically sidestepped it, unless we were extremely competitive, or had serious perfectionist parents.

Up to this point there were too many other things competing for our attention to give dance lessons a second thought. When there was a pause for consideration it was too late. There was the ever present thought of embarrassment by crushing a toe, or ruining a favorite shoe by stepping on your partner's foot, or just simply not knowing what to do and getting laughed at by others who suppose they did. So you and your beau gingerly walked onto the dance floor and wiggled, gyrated and flailed around self-consciously, smiling ridiculously, trying to make those awesome moves relatively in time with the music; all the while looking around to see how everyone else was doing it, hoping that what you had going on didn't look too out of place.

Then the music suddenly stopped and was instantly replaced by a slow one. You were stuck now, nowhere to go. You thought you saw an encouraging look from your partner, or at least a pleasant resignation and you moved into each other's arms and stumbled around awkwardly for a couple of minutes, feigning actual enjoyment. Yes, it was exciting to have your arms around someone of the opposite sex, but the idea was to be dancing, and this was a poor imitation.

In our mind's eye what we had really envisioned was to be the best dancer on the floor, unconscious of our steps and body movements, totally absorbed in the moment with someone we really liked. The Prom or another dance party was the hopeful search for an experience that matched our romantic teenage expectations. For whatever reason, our wishful thinking was seldom fully realized. It was fun to be sure. The memory is forever etched in our conscious mind, but it was still far short of what we had conjured up in our all too vivid imaginations.

On some level that's what it's like when we try to live our daily lives in the spirit. The thought of it is exciting and yet our expectations are never fully realized; partially because we are not sure of what we are supposed to experience, and partly because what we did experience could potentially have been attributed to so many other random things that we had no absolute confirmation that we actually accomplished anything "in the spirit." Maybe it was just us doing "our thing."

Another element of it is that we've seldom seen demonstrated what it means to be a disciple of Christ operating in the dunamis power of the Holy Spirit on a continuing basis. Yes, we've read a few books, seen a few videos and heard a few stories about the lives of a few powerful saints that gave us some insight, but most of those were only third party observations of the men and women who led remarkable lives under the anointing of the Lord (in some foreign country) – yet there are so few first person accounts available to measure ourselves by.

Then too, the books we've read and the stories we've heard of daring-do and feats of miracles from far-flung foreign lands were strung together as if they happened every day, when they may only happed a hand full of times over a 20 year period. So even in that we may have something we can aspire to, but still don't have a firm model we can look to, especially for those of us who live in a modern work-a-day world.

This is one more reason why we as parents and elders in the body of Christ need to be very frank and honest with those coming up behind us. They need some evidence that the things they've heard from others is actually real in our own lives as well, that God is engaged with us in all of it, and as such it can be emulated.

Sooner or later, those who follow us will come to the same place as Elisha did after Elijah left the planet in an angelic chariot; he picked up Elijah's fallen mantle, walked to the Jordan River and smacked the surface of the water with the mantle and yelled, "Where is the God of Elijah?" They have to see it operating in us first.

This is one of the main reasons that God chose Abraham to do such spectacular things in his behalf;

Genesis 18:19 *"For I know him, **that he will command his children and his household after him**, and they shall keep the way of the LORD, to do justice and judgment; that the LORD may bring upon Abraham that which he hath spoken of him."*

The phrase, "Dance Like You Mean It" generally conjures up one of two images. The first is specific dance with a number of predictable steps and moves, along with a specific genre of music such that each is unforgettably tied to the other, such as a waltz or a samba. The other image is akin to a combination of wild uninhibited dance scenes from the movies *Dirty Dancing* and *Michael*, all done to the song Footloose by Kenny Loggins.

This little treatise is intended to reframe a few things for you so that as you can begin your dance with some helpful background and some firmer expectation.

What we collectively will have to do is allow the Lord to change our way of seeing and hearing. But we cannot make that transition until we make the decision to do so, and do it with the firm conviction, and that it is important to do so quickly.

So let's get into it.

3

Your Human Spirit Makeup

In Genesis Chapter One we see that God created man and woman in His image, then in John Chapter 4 we hear Jesus say that God is a spirit and that the only way we can worship Him is in spirit and truth. Without diving in to focus on worship, let's look at the foundational message being presented here; you and I were created first and foremost as spirit beings. That viewpoint was reinforced by the Apostle Paul later in his life when he penned a letter to the Thessalonians;

> *"And the very God of peace sanctify you wholly; and I pray God your whole spirit and soul and body be preserved blameless unto the coming of our Lord Jesus Christ." (1 Thessalonians 5:23)*

In the above noted passage Paul lays out for us a mini-brief regarding how are created, and presents to us the order in which we should live; our human spirit in subjection to Holy Spirit, which in turn should rule over our soul (mind, will and emotions) which should then rule over our physical body.

Then there a couple of other interesting references to our human spirits noted in the closing verses of 2 Timothy and the letter written by Onesimus, a servant of Paul.

> *"The Lord Jesus Christ be with thy spirit. Grace be with you. Amen." (2 Timothy 4:22)*

> *"The grace of our Lord Jesus Christ be with your spirit. Amen." (Written from Rome to Philemon) (Philemon 1:25)*

Generally speaking, the only concrete understanding we have about the human spirit is recognized when we go to a funeral. We look into the casket upon the corpse of the one we knew and observe that there's nobody home and all the lights are out. The spirit of the person has obviously departed to realms unknown. That we get. But we don't stop to think that when we greet a friend on the street that the spirit of that person is sustaining the life we are encountering and completely animating it in a fashion that is uniquely recognizable as the one we've come to know and appreciate. But, there's more to it than just that.

Since the writers of the New Testament apparently knew some secrets about the presence and function of the human spirit, (noted in the verses above) and considered it important enough to stress, we probably have to learn how to function as spirit beings as well.

Let me add one more piece of information to your knowledge for your consideration. In Jeremiah 1:4-5 we read;

> *4 "Now the word of the LORD came to me, saying,*

> 5 <u>Before I formed you</u> in the womb I <u>knew</u> you, and before you were born I **consecrated** you; I **appointed** you a prophet to the nations."

The intimation of these verses is that somewhere in pre-recorded history you and I existed, probably as spirits, prior to our tour of duty here on earth in a body of flesh and bone.

I believe that this was more than us being just some abstract thought in the fertile mind of God because the word translated as 'knew" is the same word used when Adam 'knew' Eve and she conceived a son. To me it points to much more than mere intellectual knowledge of us and declares that there was some sort of intimate relationship between us – spirit to spirit. I believe that this is one of the reasons even primitive man has always sought for God and somehow intrinsically knew there was a grand creator, even as the American Indian acknowledged the Great Spirit, for there was a faint residual memory of personal connection to Him that cried out for a daily restoration of it.

Like Jeremiah, we came into this world in a tiny body, with a brain that was still in the process of being formed. We had to cognitively learn what all those things were that we could see and touch meant; we had no pre-existing grid for it because this was our first introduction to it. We didn't have or need all this additional equipment before.

Our human spirit, however, was different in that it was fully functional in the womb and fully formed where we arrived, it just didn't have anything it could operate through (a fully formed brain.) When we arrived, we were so overwhelmed by the physical and emotional sensory input of our body and developing soul, that the development of our human spirit was left in the dust, preferring to give all our time, attention and effort to the development of our knowledge base. The system of the world started in earnest in training us how to function in this domain only, apart from the spirit.

So we have come to see, hear, and process all that input through a brain that has been trained by the system of this world. So it is no wonder that hearing with spiritual ears and seeing with spiritual eyes is so foreign to us. And this doesn't even speak to the issue of interpreting through our five senses the input from the spiritual dimension with also live in. There are so few folk who even know anything about it that, much less operate in it proficiently, that it's easy to forget about it and go on with life as we have been taught to know it, oblivious to what else is available to us.

And this is really sad because when someone encounters a person who is really in touch with Holy Spirit it appears that he or she has simply disconnected from the world, which to the observer is interpreted that this person has disconnected the majority of the capacities and capabilities of their soul.

But there is something undeniable within us that whispers, "there is more." We've stuffed it down over the years and muted it as best we can, but the message is still there. It will never be snuffed out because it is how we were created; to hear things other don't, can't or refuse to hear; to see things others will never look into; to somehow know things others will never have a perception of; to perceive things that others will never choose to recognize.

We refer to that as being supernatural! That word seems to engender the idea of super heroes and not something attainable for each of us. But it's actually very natural for you to be supernatural. It's the way you were created. You just have to decide it's what you want and that it's worth the trouble to learn how to walk in all that you were created to engage. For whatever reason, we simply chose to do it naturally as children but gave it up as adults.

I don't remember going through the pro's and con's of walking or running, before deciding to try it. Do you? No, it looked cool, everyone was doing it, and it might enhance our independence, so we just did it.

This is no different. Yes, you will crawl before you walk, then you will likely walk and stumble around and fall a few times before you learn to run hesitantly. But before you know it you'll be cruising to wherever you want to go. You just need to choose to take the first steps.

Now before we move on, I need to say a few things to those of you who grew up seeing and feeling things in the spirit and still do. Like anything else, you have these "giftings" whether you like it or not. To some this "gifting" has become difficult to live with because you feel everybody's junk, you are impacted by any negative spiritual atmosphere you happen to bump into and you read people's issues before they even know what they are … and you don't like it because you can't seem to control it and the preponderance of it is emotionally overwhelming.

I will address that in a later chapter and I will help learn how you can not only come to grips with it all, but how to mature to a place where you can live with it productively.

4

Some Exercises to Familiarize You with Your Human Spirit

In order to help you make the transition to living out of your spirit you are going to have to intentionally do some things you haven't done before, and you are going to have to do it with some regularity in order to have any degree of success in it.

First of all you are going to have to understand that there are three voices you need to be aware of. They are the voice of the devil, the voice of the Holy Spirit and your own voice.

1) The voice of the devil you are probably already familiar with. It's the negative one, the one that suggests to you that you're not _____ (whatever), or that you can't _____, or you should "give that person a piece of your mind" when you darn well know you shouldn't. It's the voice of the accuser.
2) The voice of the Holy Spirit is probably the one that you have confused with your conscience on occasion. It is the quiet voice, one that is softer than a whisper, sometimes it is more recognized as a "knowing" rather than a hearing. With practice it will become a voice with

spoken words. It is also the Spirit that brings us a "check: when we're about to make a bad choice.
3) The third voice is yours. It's not the one that makes you utter a cuss word when you mess up. It's the one that says I want to do this when dreams of the heart are at stake.

Here's a simple exercise for you ... Go stand on the sidewalk in the busiest part of town the place where there are numerous pedestrians, or a college campus when classes change. Put on sunglasses and close your eyes, carry a small open book as though you are intent on reading it so that those passing by are not distracted by you, nor you by them. If you don't wear sunglasses, stand on a sidewalk facing a reflective wall, preferably a store window. Then listen for footsteps on the sidewalk as they pass by behind you.

Take a couple of deep breaths, relax and tell your human spirit to become active and see if you can determine the sex of each passerby. You can check your guess in the window reflection as they pass by. Try not make your choice based upon the sound their footwear makes, or the sound of their voice if they are speaking on the phone or to a companion with them, even though that will be difficult to ignore. (Even when it's a self-imposed exercise it's hard not to want to do well.)

Then write down your score. Keep it for comparison for the next outing.

If there happens to be someone whose gate is uneven, is limping or walking with a cane, in addition to their sex, ask the Holy Spirit what their issue is and check it in the reflection. Pray for them if urged to do so.

On one of your next outings try guessing what color shirt or blouse they are wearing as they walk by. You will be surprised at how accurate you will become because the sensitivity to your spirit is rising.

This exercise is how you can begin to walk out Hebrews 5:14

> *"But strong meat belongeth to them that are of full age, even those who by reason of use have their senses exercised to discern both good and evil."*

Most of you just flunked the scriptural interpretation and understanding test because you chose as the subject of this sentence to "discern both good and evil" because that's how a mind steeped in the system of the world would process it.

It is discernment, but it is not based on what you know or can figure out from past experience. No, it's your God-given senses – your five senses; smell, taste, touch, sight, hearing ..... plus your spiritual senses that have to be trained to discern good and evil. You are going to have to activate that portion of your being, otherwise you're going to get nowhere. So get intentional about it.

We have used our five senses to try to 'figure out' what is good for us, or perhaps it's better said as 'won't harm us' and to isolate ourselves from what may be troublesome to us; extreme heat and freezing cold, sharp knives and pointed objects, great heights and flood waters, getting fired or demoted, including the worst of all, rejection and embarrassment. How is it that we have failed to use those same five senses to determine if something is either good or evil? It is because the system of the world (created by the enemy himself) never wanted you to learn it, for obvious reasons. They have been relegated to self-protection.

I always have a great deal more success when praying for people for healing, or when doing land cleansing, when I can touch the person, the structure or the soil. I don't necessarily "feel" anything spiritually or physically, but I know the results are much better when I do.

We were out in Texas sometime back doing land cleansing on a large piece of partially developed property. It had been a while since I had been in Texas and a great while since I had done any land cleansing in Texas. I put my hand out and leaned on a large pin oak tree as is my norm, and immediately I heard, "Welcome home." Now I don't know for sure if what I heard was from the Holy Spirit, the tree, or the land, but being born, married, all my grandparents are buried there, and deciding to follow Jesus – all in Texas – I suspect it was definitely one of the first two.

Let's look at some other common examples.

If you have bought this book, you are at an age to have had the experience of meeting someone you immediately didn't like or were instantly suspicious of. At the time you didn't know why, for some unknown reason you just didn't really like or trust them. Over time you have tried to hone in on why? Was it simply their looks you didn't like? Did they remind you of someone else who did you wrong? Have you begun to stereotype? Do you have specific prejudices about people and how they look or act? Or was it really your discernment of good and evil kicking in? We've all been through that inquisition. Sometimes we were proven right and sometimes we were all wrong about them. But more often than not, we were proven right.

On the other hand, we've all had the experience of having someone tell us something negative about another person only to get to know them later and find out that what was said was not only inaccurate, but couldn't have been further from the truth. In fact, they turned out to be not only really likable people, but incredibly valuable to know. How is it that we have no discernment in these situations? Why is it easier to believe bad reports from or about people without even knowing them?

Here's an exercise for you;

Try this when you are in a new city window shopping, or for that matter in your home town, or visiting shop after shop as you stroll through the main drag of a tourist destination. Do you occasionally walk into a shop that gives you the 'willies,' rubs you the wrong way, gives you the creeps, feels bad, or in some way makes you feel very uncomfortable? It happens to us all periodically, and it happens with me quite often.

There are three possibilities for your reaction;

> 1) the ownership of the store, or its employees are heavily into the occult, and the presence of evil is palpable, or
>
> 2) the store carries a great deal of new age and/or occult associated items, which has attracted familiar spirits, or
>
> 3) either the building itself is defiled, or the land it sits on is heavily defiled.

Either way, my wife and I will pick up on it within four or five seconds of entry, forcing us to make a hasty retreat. Often times we don't even stop to see which of the three it is, we just leave.

I seldom even stop to see if I can address it unless halted by the Holy Spirit and given instructions on what to do. (Jesus didn't deal with every demon he saw, and He could identify them all. He only dismissed the ones that were between Him and what the Father wanted Him to accomplish.)

I always wind up leaving any store where incense is burning, not because it is evil, and it may well be, but I leave because my sinuses can't stand it.

However, if this sort of thing should happen to you, before you walk away from the shop, see if you can determine what the source of your discomfort is. Stop for 30 seconds and inquire of Holy Spirit. There is a difference among them that is worth noting. Do you feel like there is something you can pray into in order to deal with the defilement on the property for the sake of the owners and their patrons? We'll address authority in a bit.

Here's another one you might want to consider;

You walk into a restaurant for dinner looking forward to a great meal because you've heard a lot of positive comments about this place. The dining room is almost full and the host or hostess escorts you to a table, pulls out a chair and motions for you to be seated there. But somehow you instinctively feel like that is not only not the chair you're supposed to sit in, but it's not even the table you are supposed to sit at.

Often times we balk at thinking that these are "natural" responses to these situations simply because we don't want to sit with our back to the entire dining room unable to see anything. So we just sit down slightly perturbed reasoning that there's nothing else available because the dining room is almost full and we don't want to make a scene. But more often than not there is something else going on that we are not in tune with that makes us uncomfortable and desiring to sit elsewhere.

Here's another one you might be familiar with:

Have you ever been looking for a house to buy or rent and as you drove by the curb appeal of the place either didn't put you off nor really appeal to you either, but when you parked and got out of the car things began to change? The corner lot was fine. It was spacious, had a couple of mature trees, and the neighborhood looked and felt good as you drove in. However, in walking up to the house it just started to feel odd, it didn't feel right. Something was definitely off, but it wasn't immediately apparent what it was.

As you stood in the yard, the house itself appeared structurally sound. The house had obviously been well maintained. The roofing looked relatively new, the materials and the finishes were pleasing, and the colors were attractive. The yard was manicured, and everything seemed in order but ... something still just didn't feel right. What was it?

Then as you started to walk around the side of the house it suddenly hit you what it was. The house was facing in the wrong direction. It didn't fit the lot.

How was it that this was such a problem for you when no one else seemed to be remotely bothered by it? The answer is that you have sensitivity to the land itself. Land always has flow and the direction the house is facing must be in alignment with it in order for everything to be in proper order. The Chinese call it Feng Shui, which claims to use energy forces to harmonize individuals with their surrounding environment. That's weird.

Since you and I were created in the image of God, and the raw materials He used to create us with was dirt, and His first command to us was to take care of and steward the earth ... is it possible that you are more closely connected to the earth than you are aware of?

I am not advocating that we should go about judging people, their businesses or how their property is situated, but we do it automatically anyway when being around something that makes us feel uncomfortable. We usually just write it off to conventional wisdom, or bad luck to be where we are. There is a world of difference between judgment and discernment. We need to make a distinction regarding something we are sensing to determine if this is something we are picking up on spiritually, or is it the product of something else. What I'm after here is this: How do we get to the point where we come to recognize and trust each of the various feelings and signals we get as being spiritual discernment when we absolutely have to? When it actually may be a matter of life and death!

The only way to do it is found in the verse you just read –

> *"... by reason of use (practice) have their senses exercised (trained) to discern..."*

Maturity or proficiency in doing anything comes only from doing it – frequently. Yes, in the process of learning you will make mistakes and feel like you made a fool of yourself on occasion. That's part of the price that maturity requires you to pay. But you don't want to have to crawl all your life when you have your sights set on running. You just have to negotiate the steps in between and pay the price for it.

I can hear some of you now saying, "this is all new age BS and none of this should matter to Bible believing Christians at all because they never taught this sort of stuff in Sunday School and I can't find it anywhere in the Bible. If it had been important they would have mentioned it to us. Besides, we were warned about living from our feelings!"

My response is very simple. God said that everything He made was "good." (His words, not mine.) So if He created us with these feelings and emotions, these nudges, checks and these sensory perceptions, who am I to say they are bad and should be ignored? It's generally not very good to be in disagreement with God.

Others would say, the only reason to engage with this sort of thing is that you're trying to gain a competitive edge, just to keep from being wounded or being taken advantage of. My answer is, Yes Sir! Scripture says,

> "therefore be wise as serpents and harmless as doves." (Matthew 10:16) and

> "A wise man will hear, and will increase learning; and a man of understanding shall attain unto wise counsels:" (Proverbs 1:5)

Is this not a portion of what walking by the spirit is about? Learning to trust the nudges, the checks, and the questions?

Only a fool blows off a warning and intentionally walks into a buzz-saw expecting to emerge unscathed. But then, I suppose this is why every hospital has built Surgical Centers and Emergency Rooms.

So how do we get there? We are going to have to start paying attention to our entire body, our emotions, physical sensations, checks in out spirit, portions of our body vibrating, smells and tastes, anything that is different than it was a few moments ago. There might be 50 different levels of emotion between a slight feeling that something's not right, and all out fun-for-your-life terror. But we need to be able to understand what those are, how they feel and put an accurate name on it. If there is no difference in feeling frustrated and murderous anger, what will you always react to?

You are going to have to become self-aware.

Do you realize that if you are not in touch with your emotions then you will have very little discernment at all? If you leave all processing to your brain, when times get tough, you're screwed because you'll have no idea who is friend or foe, what is dangerous and what isn't, and have no access to a strategy to deal with either one appropriately.

5

First Things First

One of the major reasons we can't see what we ought to be seeing, hear what need to hear and dance like we want to dance is that we have intentionally chosen not to see or hear, and our dance is a copy of someone else's (typically what the world says is appropriate.)   We have naturally chosen to zero in a signal that is not the one were created to connect on. Just like your television, you have to select the right channel to view what you want to watch. If you want to watch the Super Bowl game, you won't get to see it on the Home Shopping Network channel. You have to make a change.

Fortunately, God made us with a multi-channel receiver, one which we can choose to tune in with, tune out, or completely turn off. We just have to make the choice.

It all begins with intentionality. If you do not intentionally choose to see differently, and hear differently, even think differently, nothing will ever change for you. It really is that simple. "Do nothing," is always a viable option when contemplating a logical response to any stimulus, or opportunity. Yet if you want to live with purpose, or dance like you really mean it, doing nothing is not really an option.

When you were a child the only way to learn to walk or run was to try it. There were bumps and bruises along the way, but the act of walking and running was well worth the price we paid. Speaking of intentionality ... how many of you have taken the time to thank your parents for teaching you to walk and then to run? Or for that matter, how about the potty training thing they took you through. Now there's a skill that's come in real handy over the years? The point of it is that we were created to do some things naturally (replace with supernaturally if you wish) because that's the way it was intended all along. But we have to learn to operate in them.

When we moved from Asheville, NC to Campbellsville, KY a few years ago we landed in a community that does one of the most meaningful things we've ever been privileged to be a part of called Declaration Dinners. Each December we individually spend time searching our hearts and the Lord's heart for what we would like to have achieved (naturally and spiritually) by midnight on December 31st of the following year.

For the balance of December and into early January, you were to take you list before the Lord and ask Him to alter it in any way He so chooses. Having made the alterations, if any, we then bring our list to a lavish dinner in some time in January.

The group of ten to twelve that we were a part of shared a fine catered dinner together, usually accompanied by a case of wine. At the conclusion of the dinner, everyone fills their glass, and each individual (or couple if they are written that way) stands and declares what they are going to achieve in the succeeding 12 months. This is followed immediately by a group toast, a hearty Amen, prophetic words and prayer, then the next individual reads their declarations.

Lest some of you think that this is just some gross display of narcissism, do you remember the verses that go,

> "*Delight yourself in the Lord and He will give you the* **desires of your heart**." (Psalms 37:4)

> Proverbs 18:21 "*Death and life are in the power of the tongue: and they that love it shall eat the fruit thereof.*"

> "**at the mouth of two witnesses,** *or at the mouth of three witnesses, shall the matter be established.*" Deuteronomy 19:15b (KJV)

I believe that when God created each of us He put into our being (identity) a set of desires that were commensurate with our purpose for being here. Without that specific set of desires you and I would never be drawn to the destiny, or purpose for which we were created. Therefore, many, if not all of the desires we bring to our declaration dinners were actually directly from the heart of God deposited eons ago.

> Proverbs 10:24 "*The fear of the wicked, it shall come upon him:* **but the desire of the righteous shall be granted.**"

The wisdom of this act is incredibly profound. First of all, there is the soul searching that goes on in preparation, allowing God to weigh in on what we set our hearts to do, even allowing Him to reorder our priorities. I believe that this is the manner that we should always live, being intentional about what we are doing and where we are going with our lives, mindful that God may want to re-direct it toward more important Kingdom pursuits.

> "The steps of a *good* man are ordered by the LORD: and he delighteth in his way." Psalms 37:23 (KJV)

Do you want to build something important? Count the cost, as the scripture says. This process prioritizes the next year what you will pray about, prepare for, save and sacrifice for. It determines what other activities you will push aside because they can't compete with the greater thing you have chosen to give yourself to. It automatically determines where you will spend your resources and your energy. This is dancing like you mean it.

Our God is a god of order. Declarations establish order in your life.

The process also makes room for others in your life; people who can hold you accountable to achieve the things you want to achieve and grants them access to your private world by allowing them permission to inquire about your progress, or even question the wisdom of your choices during the following year. It also opens the door for cooperation on their part to help you achieve your goals. It is another of the vital elements necessary for in a life giving community – dance partners if you will.

It is also a very spiritual endeavor. God created us in His image, and the manner in which He created everything but humans on this earth was through His voice – He spoke things into existence. We are to do the same.

Nothing happens in the earth unless we declare it. It activates angels to begin working to set things in order for their accomplishment. It activates the Holy Spirit to work in our hearts, minds and daily affairs to bring it about, and to bring those around us who are supposed to be part of it so that what we give ourselves to comes to fruition. Without our voice speaking things into existence nothing happens.

If you have had a great idea and did not speak it into the atmosphere, neither you, nor anyone else was ever able to accomplish it because angels were never activated to perform it. Many of the great ideas you've had came directly from God. Some of them were meant for you to do. Some of them are meant for others to do. But no one will pick them up and do them unless you speak them into existence ... just because you had ears to hear. You are the chosen conduit. Don't choke the flow of blessing and progress into the earth.

> "The heavens are the Lord's heavens, and the earth He has given into the hands of men." Psalms 115:16

In other words, God may have numerous desires that He would like to have accomplished here on earth; inventions that heal, solutions to massive problems enacted, books that need to be written, speeches that need to be given, songs that need to be sung, art that must be painted and sculpted, plays and poems written, etc, etc, etc. but none of them will see the light of day without someone speaking them into existence.

In the year following our initial Declaration Dinner we were able to accomplish 9 of the 11 items we declared on our list. One of the goals I announced a couple of years ago was that I wanted more joy in my life. In order to achieve that goal Holy Spirit showed me that I had to re-order some of the things I was giving my attention to. So the Lord began to put His finger on things that needed to change. I had to cancel subscriptions to some blogs and newsletters I had subscribed to because they were feeding me such negativity, voluntarily robbing me of joy. That likely would not have happened had I not made the decision, and the declaration, of wanting more joy in my life. Does that mean I need to be uninformed? No, it simply means that I needed to tune my receiver differently; cut out some of the noise that has been robbing me of joy.

Intentionality is everything. Without it nothing happens, and certainly nothing changes for the better.

All that being said ...

6

What am I after?

Since you are first and foremost a spirit being, you are going to have to begin to start relating to life as such – you have to begin acting like it! You can only do that intentionally because you were not brought up in this world by the tenants of the Kingdom. You have been totally indoctrinated in the principles of this tangible world, and the two are at odds with one another. That's one of the reasons why Matthew 6 ends with this charge … *"seek first the Kingdom of God …"*

You are going to have to un-learn a number of things- - then intentionally key in on Kingdom ideas, principles and paradigms of thought. You can't do it any other way.

One of the reasons we enjoyed operating healing rooms so much is that it intentionally put us in the position that if God didn't show up and do something for someone, we would look like idiots. When you intentionally put yourself in a place where God has to show up, it's not testing God at all, He loves to show up in behalf of those who desperately need him because they have no other options.

That's the function of priests (that's you and me) before the Lord, bringing the needs of others before the throne of Grace in their time of need. God certainly will not show up if your motive is to enhance your ego or show someone that you're more spiritual than they. But God likes to show up in behalf of those who are trusting Him and Him alone.

> "For the eyes of the LORD run to and fro throughout the whole earth, to give strong support to those whose heart is blameless toward him." 2 Chronicles 16:9

The Healing Rooms was one of our greatest exercises in intentionality – about 30 to 40 people every Thursday evening for nine years.

Here's another exercise for you. A friend of ours in Atlanta decided that he needed to exercise his sprit and being led by the Spirit as he began to inquire of the Holy Spirit to guide him to the dwelling of friends he had lost contact with over the years. (This was just before phones with GPS in them became common.) The challenge was that he had no phone number and couldn't even be assured that they still lived in the Atlanta area. So he would get into his car, go to the end of the driveway and ask, "Which way do I turn to go see my friend Bill? " If he felt, heard or sensed that it was 'right,' then he turned 'right,' and so on till he arrived as his destination. He said many times he would get lost and have to turn around and go home, but on numerous occasions he found his way to the new home of someone he hadn't seen in years.

God will meet you in these spiritual experiments because it is His desire that you grow in your gifting, as well as in confidence that He is able to guide you and direct you perfectly.

Back in 1985 while I was still working as a Marketing and Sales Director for an industrial manufacturer, and also working part time for Derin Carmack's ministry in Northern Colorado, I started seeing angels at church for the first time. (And mind you I was pushing 40 years of age at the time.) At first they were only visible when someone would get saved in a Sunday morning service, when each person was escorted down the aisle by three or four small flying angelic beings, similar to cherubs; each totally white, quasi-trans parent and only about 30 inches tall. They laughed and giggled all the way. On other occasions it was a much larger sword-wielding angel that stood on the corner of the platform when our pastor, or a special speaker spoke or ministered. It happened on most Sundays for about 18 months.

When 1987 rolled in, a major recession hit the US and its effects ramped up quickly on the Front Range in Colorado. The owner of the company I was with freaked out because on paper he'd lost half of his assets in the stock market, coupled with a major theft by an employee of another company he'd been a partner in years before. He came in one Monday and let 30% of his employees go, including me. IBM shrank, government contracts with Front Range high tech firms began to dry up, but fared better than most. Seagate, who at the time was the largest manufacturer of computer disc drives in the world, quickly felt the downturn in sales and let go 5,200 employees one Friday afternoon, driving the local unemployment rate to greater than 25 percent.

After a year of finding nothing in the remnants of my own industry and no other viable prospects across the country, I got mad at God. That ended my visibility of angels.

It didn't get reactivated until 2003 when a dear friend of ours took us to a Dr. Paul Cox (Aslansplace.com) training in Elizabeth City, NC. It was at the time the strangest thing I'd ever been to. By Tuesday afternoon I wasn't sure I wanted to enjoy the rest of it. But our host had driven us across the State to attend the training, so we couldn't leave. That was God's doing. Not only were my spiritual eyes opened again, but I began to see much more than that. His training was indispensable in educating us in many aspects of the spirit realm, along with the fact that there are so many other Godly beings, all of whom seem to have specific assignments and functions.

I think it's important to note that between '87 and '03 I was having occasional dreams from the Lord, seeing images of places, things, and interactions with Jesus off and on throughout this whole period. Sometimes it was to tell me how to pray, Sometimes it was Jesus engaging me personally because of where I was at the time. I just never saw angelic activity again until that training event in '03. What is the significance of that? I think it had much to with personal choice, for there are consequences to our choices, even if they are unintended.

2003 was when we began inviting angels to join us in ministering to individuals who had come in from out of town for prayer ministry. This doesn't happen every time we minister, but it's often enough to keep us open to the option. (Hebrews 1:14) Engaging the real thing also helps you recognize the bad guys when they show up, which they do on occasion – and that makes it really easy to dispense with them.

As for seeing with spirit eyes, hopefully this next story will give you some idea of how important it has become to me.

We had moved from Asheville, NC to Campbellsville, KY in late August of 2011. We were doing the last of a series of two-day Inner Healing RoundTables around the country where we invited the principals from six to eight different ministries (tools or programs) that we found to be key in establishing a comprehensive healing community, similar to what we had built in Asheville. They would spend 60 to 90 minutes talking about the ministry, what tools they used, who it was directed toward and how to get trained in it. It put a couple of those ministries on the map and greatly expanded the ministry of the others.

We were doing one in Nashville, TN in the late Spring of 2012 when I started to experience significant physical discomfort. I am usually the last speaker on Saturday afternoon and by the time it was my turn, I was really struggling.

When we got home I immediately went to my local physician who referred me to a specialist. The bottom line is that I was diagnosed with colon cancer which required surgery quickly. As you might imagine, I was shocked at the pronouncement. A day or two later I asked the Lord, "Am I gonna be alright?" thinking of the short term situation with surgery, and of the longer term issue of dealing with cancer. Both my parents had died of cancer. My dad's bone cancer was a recurrence of an earlier bout with prostate cancer.

His response to my question dealt with all my angst. *"Some of this you're gonna like. Some of it you're not. But I'll be with you though it all."* My fear and concerns evaporated instantly.

The surgery went well and I am now the proud owner of a semi-colon. The downside was that what was supposed to be a 3 hour surgical procedure turned out to be a five–and-a-half hour marathon event. (I guess those guys get paid by the hour.) The real downside was when the anesthesia wore off I was left with a major case of neuropathy in both arms. Any time I moved either hand in a backhanded motion, even a couple of inches, a searing pain would start at the knuckle of my index finger and run up my arm to my shoulder. The pain was so sharp and so intense that it would literally take my breath away. I would be absolutely frozen for three or four seconds.

Apparently, my neck was not well supported on the articulated table used during the surgery and over 5.5 hours, vertebrae C3 and C4 were disturbed significantly and it still gives me problems occasionally, now eight years later.

While in the hospital my chiropractor and friend Dr. Ray Roberts came to see me and I explained to him my dilemma. His response was, Get to me as soon as you can because if we can't fix this within about 30 days you are going to be stuck with most it for life. Well, that was incentive enough for me!

As soon as I could I marched myself down to his office and he took an x-ray of my neck. He told me to lie down on the adjustment table and moved off into the corner to review the x-ray. What Ray didn't know, but I did, was about seven or eight years earlier I had my first (and last) encounter with a chiropractor. He cracked (adjusted) my neck and I hurt for about six weeks afterward. I made a firm vow that I would never do that again! So here I was, between the proverbial rock and a hard place, needing to deal with the pain from the neuropathy, but afraid I was going to have to endure constant neck pain as a result of trying to deal with it … and possibly be paralyzed in the bargain.

That's when He showed up – Jesus, that is.

He stood between Ray and I facing me, hand clasped together, excitedly jumping up and down like a little kid on Christmas morning. He was absolutely thrilled that Ray and I were together working on my problem. He never said a word, but the smile on His face was so big it almost glowed.

As quickly as He had come, He was gone ... and so was all my angst about the adjustment.

Over the next few months the pain subsided a bit as I went to my local Chiropractor, but it was not gone when I went in for my first CT Scan following the surgery.

It was early Summer time and it was a warm day. I made the mistake of wearing shorts and a T-shirt. I say 'mistake' because they keep those CT machines down in the refrigerated section of the basement and they are manned by very cold-blooded people. In order to get the contrast they want, you have to drink a bunch of nasty tasting stuff that vaguely tastes like 3 pounds of chalk dissolved in orange flavored tang, with a dose of radiator fluid. (If you're too young to know what Tang was count yourself lucky. It came out about the same time as margarine and was touted as a product of the space race.) Following the ingestion of that vile tasting liquid compound, patients have to sit around in a separate meat locker for another 45 minutes looking at three year old home decorating magazines, while some nearby lady blabbers on about aunt Martha's incontinence issues, while some TV talk show is playing on a television whose sound or channel selection you cannot control.

Finally they bring you into "the room." Apparently these people have several layers of clothing underneath their tidy hospital scrubs because their teeth didn't chatter with the cold like mine did, nor were their lips blue like mine. You couldn't tell that the cold got to them at all. Then the lady with the needle comes in to administer the radioactive juice they inject immediately before they run you through the CT machine. They may not be cold, but you figure out real quick that you are close to freezing because your veins are now shrunken to barely detectable levels due to the approaching hypothermia.

This did not deter this young lady with the needle one bit for she poked around like a driller stricken with 'black gold fever' till she found the red fountain she was looking for. The problem is that the University of Louisville Hospital is a teaching hospital and they apparently break in all their students on patients getting a CT scan. (It's either that or they pull innocent homeless drug addicts who have experience with needles off the street promising them a clean dry bed and free lunch in the cafeteria.) What this young lady lacked in skill, she made up for in perseverance.

Now one of the interesting things about this particular CT machine was that it was apparently an older model, or one specifically made for skinny people, for the narrow platform I had to lay on to go in and out of the scanner was only about 13 inches wide. My shoulders, and other undisclosed portions of my anatomy, however are much wider leaving no room on the platform for my arms to rest on. Houston, We have a problem.

Rather than leaving your hands and arms free to get hung up in the gearing that drives the platform you are lying on, the protocol is to take a three inch wide belt and strap your wrists to your upper thighs. This the attendants accomplished with great gusto. She did thankfully refrain from putting her foot on my thigh as she cinched me up like a saddle on a horse, with some force.

Once cinched in, I heroically held back both my tears and screams until she finally found a place to administer the 'juice,' pushed the plunger and began the process of running me in and out of the fun-house magnetic tunnel three times.

Admittedly, I was already miserable before the scan began, what with being a near-frozen pin cushion for a student nurse and now having the circulation to my hands cut off, but apparently my neck was no longer in an appropriate position for the ride either and the neuropathy I had previously experienced was returning, propelled by throbbing in my hands.

About midway through the second trip in and out of the scanner the searing pain was back again and it was marching up my arm in time with the beat of my heart. It didn't take long for it to escalate way beyond uncomfortable and the growing intensity of it made me think I couldn't make it through the third and last trip in and out without making them stop. I really didn't want them to stop because I knew we'd only have to do it all over again. I certainly didn't want that! That was really bad idea – between that rock and the hard place again.

That's when He showed up – Jesus that is.

He was leaning over against the far wall, one foot pulled up against the wall, rather like the classic pose of the Marlboro man, the cowboy in the now long-gone cigarette commercial. His arms were folded across His chest and His head was cocked slightly to one side. He had a sly smirk on His face that seemed to say, "I know something you don't."

At long last He walked over to the CT machine, rested forearm on it and learned over and looked at me. Then His attention moved to the red lights spinning around because the scan was still in progress. After a long moment or two, He said, *"Well, I wouldn't have done it quite like this."* with a bit of a chuckle in His voice.

He winked at me, and then He was gone – and so was all my physical pain and fear.

Sometime later I noticed something similar in these two instances of encountering Jesus in the midst of my fear and physical pain. It finally occurred to me that while I was in the midst of these situations I had never prayed for Him to come. I never asked Him to come. I had never cried out for Him to come. I never begged for him to come. He just came … because He knew I needed Him.

Let that sink in a bit.

Scripture tells us to *"Cast all your cares in Him for He cares for you"* (1Peter 5:7) which sorta makes it all about us appropriately responding to Him in hopes of gaining access to His comfort. But it also says that He's the friend who sticks closer than a brother, (Proverbs 18:24) and a *"brother is born for adversity"* (Proverbs 17:17) in other words, to help you through yours. So why wouldn't He come?

He also said this in John 15:13-16a,

> 13 *"Greater love hath no man than this, that a man lay down his life for his friends.*
> *14 You are my friends, if you do whatever I command you.*

> *15 Henceforth I no longer call you servants; for the servant doesn't know what his Master is doing: but **I have called you friends**; for I have made known unto you everything that I have heard from my Father.*
> *16 **You have not chosen me, but I have chosen you**,"*

I believe that this latter experience I had with Jesus back in late 2012 was able to occur largely as the result of two activities I have given myself to.

The first is engaging (picturing) Jesus in my mind's eye using my God-given imagination (which the Lord installed in each of us.) I started doing this in the company of other believers in somewhat controlled circumstances. (Yes, our imaginations can run away with us if we are undisciplined. And Yes, I did say we can discipline our imaginations, not to go on a specific pre-programmed track, but not to run amuck by running willy-nilly where ever it wishes.)

We can read the Word of God and get information about God, but we must choose to enter into friendship in order to generate relationship. Here's a perfect example; when you were dating how did you choose to communicate? Face-to-face. You didn't go to the library and check out a book on William or Elizabeth, nor did you stalk them on Facebook. (Okay, maybe you did that.) You chose face-to-face communication because you wanted to engage all your senses to determine if you had further interest in seeing this person again.

So what were you doing? You looked to every form of human interaction. You wanted to hear the words and get a glimpse of their heart. But you also needed to hear pace, volume, intonation, vocabulary, emotion, measure their ability to express themselves, ascertain what was important to them, what they liked and didn't like, the range of their life experiences, what they hated and what they loved.

To do that we needed to also take in information visually; facial expressions, how they use their hands when emphasizing a point, a tilt of the head, the look in their eyes when they were excited or when they recalled something sad, including all the accompanying body language while speaking as well as listening.

And last, but certainly not least, what we pick up from them emotionally. Do we get them? Do they get us? Can I trust this person?

Several years ago we were at a pre-rehearsal dinner gathering prior to the wedding of my youngest daughter and I wandered around talking to all the friends of the groom, whom I had never met. Many of them had flown in to Atlanta from the West Coast for the wedding and that puzzled me because of the time and expense. There is always a time crunch to get back to a job for Monday morning when you have to travel back to the West Coast from any place east of the Mississippi, for it takes the whole blasted day. My question was, What prompted you to make this sacrifice?

Their uniform reply was delightful. A number of them had met at a boarding school. None of them had ever been there before and they knew no one. Chris (the groom) was the first person they had met. He came up and introduced himself and asked if he could show them around. As he did, Chris introduced them to a number of people, helped them find their classes and helped them get situated in their dorm. Each of them never expected to see him again after that first day, and yet he continued to be the "kindest, most selfless, most convivial person they'd ever met" for the whole time they were in school together. Consequently, they had chosen to remain connected since those days some 20 years earlier.

In order to "know" someone, we also have to be "known." To make that happen we have to meet face-to-face, first to see if I like you, then to find out enough about you so I can see if I want to know more, then learn to trust you – all of that before I can make the decision to call you my friend. Then we have to keep doing it. (No, we are not talking about Facebook friends.)

Regardless of the depth a relationship goes to, you have to spend time face-to-face with one another. So it is with becoming a friend of God. You have to spend time together. That doesn't mean reading the Bible cover to cover multiple times, although that's not a bad idea, if indeed you are reading it to discover who He is and not just for information about Him.

Here's how I started cultivating friendship with God;

Since God created us as human beings to communicate with each other through meaningful conversation; he chose the exchange of information, emotions and ideas through the use of individual words and phrases strung together to convey complete thoughts as the medium. We hear those thoughts presented to us by others and it may produce immediate understanding, conveys specific information and/or emotion, or it may produce questions about what we heard. Those questions prompt a response on our part seeking more information or to clarify understanding; hence, conversation.

So it is with God. If you are stuck in the paradigm that God only speaks through the Bible then you are missing out on a significant part of relationship. If your future wife or husband refused to speak with you, insisting that you could only get acquainted by reading a book about them, or listening to a tape they recorded, there would be a whole lot fewer marriages. Abraham, Moses and Joshua, to name a few didn't have a book to read and they did pretty well letting God speak to them, and speaking conversationally with Him in turn. We are much more fortunate, we have both.

A conversation with God can start simply by quieting yourself and asking God, "What have you got to say to me today?" then listening for His response. At the outset, you may not hear much because this is new to you. Just stay with it and it will produce fruit. Initially, write down what you think you heard.

Steve Thompson, when teaching on this subject, used to say "It's a little like a ditch after a spring rain. It's filled with sticks, leaves and twigs. But if runs for a while it will get clear." So it is with listening to the Lord. Initially some of it's our thoughts and things we project onto Him, but if we keep listening it will get clearer; more of it will be discernibly Him and less our own voice (another way to build that familiarity.) In a short, period of time you'll be writing 8 to 10 pages of things that He tells you during a single sitting.

This is where a lot of people go wrong; God tells them something and they immediately drop everything and run off to do what they thought God told them to do. Big mistake! Sit a while with Him and begin to ask questions about what He just told you. Make the questions simple, sometimes requiring only a Yes or No answer. You might even ask Him to repeat what He said in other words so that you are perfectly clear on what He just said. Just don't get in a hurry. In the long run this is about relationship, one that's incredibly good for you.

> Isaiah 46:9-11 *"Remember the former things of old: for I am God, and there is none else; I am God, and there is none like me; 10 **declaring the end from the beginning**, and from ancient times things that are not yet done; saying, My counsel shall stand, and I will do all my pleasure: 11 calling a ravenous bird from the east, the man of my counsel from a far country; yea, I have spoken, I will also bring it to pass; I have purposed, I will also do it."*

> Psalms 34:8 *"O taste and see that the **LORD is good**: blessed is the man that trusteth in him."*

> Psalms 34:10 *"The young lions do lack, and suffer hunger: but they that **seek the LORD** shall not **want any good thing**."*

In other words, God is saying, I am thoroughly good, and I set all this up from the beginning and I have a set plan (and that plan is good - Jeremiah 29:11) for what will be accomplished in the end, and nothing can keep that from being accomplished. If you will come and hang out with me, together we'll see to it that you get where both of us desire for you to go.

If you will pursue this process there is a bonus in it for you. You will discover for yourself that God desires for you to get to know Him personally. By that I mean God will reveal to you elements of Himself that you not only need to know, but few will ever discover because they never voluntarily chose to allow Him to get close enough for it to happen.

I started using this process almost 35 years ago because I had been told that prayer was somehow supposed to be a two-way conversation and I had never experienced it. I was so used to my monologue with God, which is what everybody else was told to do, that I had assumed that this was all there was, until we started attending a church and hearing from a couple of radio preachers that there was actually 'more' available to us. Finally becoming frustrated with the status quo, one day I simply said, "Lord I'm putting away my laundry list of stuff to pray about, my notepad, my daily devotional (which wasn't all that inspiring anyway), along with my daily Bible reading program; I'm not doing this anymore. I need to hear your voice. I'm just going to sit here with my pen in hand and my notebook and ask, What have you got to say to me today?"

It was intent on simply starting to write down what I believed He was going to start saying to me. Well, for some reason God doesn't like to be told what we will or won't do and what He has to do is response; He didn't say anything for four days. Thankfully, I stuck it out, then He started talking and He hasn't stopped since. Over the last 30 plus years I've learned a lot about Him just by listening; He's caring, compassionate, kind, moody, He tells it like it is and has a wonderful sense of humor, He's unbelievably attentive, gentle, yet He's firmly opinionated without being over-bearing. He's funny, wise and a great story teller, just to name a few a characteristics about Him that I've learned over the years of sitting with Him.

One of the other things I learned was that He said through Jesus that,

John 6:63 *"It is the spirit that quickeneth; the flesh profiteth nothing: the words that I speak unto you, they are spirit, and they are life."* (KJV)

As a result of Him speaking to you, stuff changes in you. I would normally begin my time with God around 3 am. I would sit with Him for between ninety minutes to a couple hours, then go back to bed before getting up and preparing for work. Normally taking two hours out of the middle of your night would make me feel like I had a hangover, groggy and not with it – not what you want when you have to be running on all cylinders at the office. But sitting with Him tended to fill me up and somehow took care of the loss of sleep. It was as though I'd gotten my normal eight hours of rejuvenating rest.

In one of those instances I was enormously surprised by what I learned. We all have our pet phrases that we feel somehow say more than the individual words themselves can convey. One day He started speaking to me and in one sentence I recognized that two of those phrases were used intentionally, except they were used in exactly the reverse order of how I normally used them – actually both phrases were backward and yet , or perhaps because of it, I could still recognize them. I was stunned. It was then I heard the Lord chuckle as He said, *"And you think I didn't notice?"*

What that said to me was unlike my earthly father, who only attended one high school sporting event that I participated in four years of football, basketball, track and baseball, my heavenly father pays enough attention to me to know how I use words and phrases. That broke a lot of things in me that I had held against my birth father, as well as God, and changed the rest of my life.

This doesn't mean that you throw away your Bible, or never turn to read and/or study it again. What it does mean is that when it comes to communication, God has not limited Himself to a book. He's so much bigger than what could possibly be contained in a single book. He even wrote in John 21:25;

> *"And there are also many other things which Jesus did, the which if they should be written every one, I suppose that even the world itself would not contain the books that should be written."*

Fast forward to December 2016; I was sitting in a chair outside our dwelling in Pemba, Mozambique awaiting the start of our day. I was mulling over my impending 70th birthday less than four months hence, wondering how many "good years" I had left. By "good years" I meant the health and energy to do what I felt that God put before me. If you've ever ridden a plane for 17.5 hours from Atlanta, GA to Johannesburg, SA you have to know that I didn't feel like I would be interested in doing that when I was 95, nor perhaps not even at 90. And then my thoughts wandered to how could I spend my remaining years to maximize the number of people I could influence. That didn't last long as the first appointment of the day showed up.

The next morning I was back out under that same tree, sitting in the same chair and the Lord surprised me by saying, *"How many good years do you want?"* I was stuck for an answer for a moment and finally blurted out, "How about 20?" His reply was, *"How about 15?"* 15 it is then. Then about an hour later I realized that I could name about three men in the Old Testament who negotiated with God for a few more or a few less of something, as Abraham did when negotiating over the destruction of Sodom and Gomorrah. I wondered, How many years did I leave on the table?

I mention this event, this one-on-one interaction, because this is the One I have come to know by virtue of intentional engagement.

I also want you to remember that God uses dreams and visions as a means of communication, perhaps as much today as He did in the first couple of chapters of Matthew to direct Joseph in his quest to protect Jesus. Visions tend to be more literally interpreted, while dreams require interpretation through understanding the symbology used in them. But either way, they are both **invitations to a conversation** because in many ways we only see in part and know in part. (1Corinthians 13:12)

I have related the foregoing stories from my journey here for several significant reasons;

You need to read stories like this to remind you that a supernatural world exists, and it is still functional today in the lives of ordinary people.

There is a place of personal friendship with God that is available to you in both the peaceful, as well as in the dark and trying times of life.

And there is still hope for those of you who have experienced horrific physical and sexual abuse, torture and torment at the hands of people you should have been able to trust, and have repeatedly cried out to God for deliverance from the effects of your experiences … and received no answer as yet.

God always sees the end from the beginning and as such has a totally different perspective for your life than you do. Our view is limited to doing what we can right now to insure that we live pain free, with no understanding or appreciation of what the struggle to be free will produce in us and through us. There is a purpose for the struggle. The conversation is needful when we can't figure out what's going on and why our prayers for relief are not immediately answered. If you'll remember his response to me was, *"Some of this you're gonna like, and some of it your're not. But I will be with you through it all."*

7

Opposing Viewpoints

I wanted to spend a few words bringing a bit of balance to what we looked into in the last couple of pages of the previous Chapter, which was tied to a couple of verses we looked at;

> Proverbs 10:24 *"The fear of the wicked, it shall come upon him: but the desire of the righteous shall be granted."*

> *"Delight yourself in the Lord and He will give you the desires of your heart."* Psalms 37:4

These verses would lead me to believe, as I have clearly stated, that the Lord put into us those things (desires) that actually tend to lead us into the very place we are to help display and build the segment of the Kingdom that we were designed to.

However, detractors have stated that this sort of view point is patently narcissistic and soon brings individuals out of the will of God into a place of selfish, self-serving spiritual disaster.

Others have said that if the pursuits of your life are not at the direction of the Lord Himself, then you are operating solely out of self will, and therefore your decisions are strictly of the flesh.

I certainly appreciate each point of view, despite the fact that there is an element of truth in each of them, I still don't agree with either of them. There are indeed times and seasons that the Lord seemingly directs every move. And there are also folks who live that way; who's stories we admire.

There are also times when we make a decision to move in one direction and the Lord either blocks it, or re-directs it completely. And this is in spite of our having sought the Lord for direction prior to making the decision. Does this make sense? Not to us, but since when has that ever been an element in God's decision making process? Never!

> Psalms 115:3 *'Our God is in the heavens; he does as he pleases." (ESV)*

I believe that all these seeming inconsistencies in the Lord's accommodation of our will, the vagaries of imposing His will from time to time, and His seeming total ambivalence at other times, are accommodated in these two scriptures;

> 1Samuel 16:7 *"But the LORD said unto Samuel, Look not on his countenance, or on the height of his stature; because I have refused him: for the LORD sees not as man sees; for man looks on the outward appearance, but the LORD looks on the heart"*

> Proverbs 16:9 *"The heart of man plans his way, but the LORD establishes his steps."*

If you believe that the Lord is in control of anything on this planet then you have to believe that He's still able to change a heart or orchestrate circumstances to cause someone to change their mind, their plans and their direction. And, by the way, He knows whether this man or woman's heart's desire is to follow the path of the Lord or not.

Part of this viewpoint is the religious belief that we must suffer for Christ and what better way to accomplish that in your life than to become a missionary and die unknown and uncared for in a mud hut in the middle of deepest, darkest Africa. The idea that God is going to make me do something I hate because it will be good for me is part of the reason that kids today are forsaking their "faith," or at least their religious upbringing, in record numbers upon entry into college.

Will we suffer as believers? Yes, we will. It doesn't take very long to figure that out. Even Jesus said, "If the world hates me, they'll hate you." So much more these days! Discipleship is laying down your life (preferences, self-will, ego, narcissistic behavior and ideologies) for the way of love, not laying down and being miserable. If that's your idea of the "Christian life," then I, like this current generation, declare that you can have all of that you want. Not me.

Jesus did not come as Emmanuel to walk me into death. He said,

> "I am come that you might have life … for I am the Way, the Truth, and the Life."

Another part of this belief is actually founded in fear imposed by the system of the world. The motivation to have God make all the decisions in your life is actually a failure avoidance motivation; "If what God tells me to do doesn't work out, then it's all His fault, not mine." It is nicely veiled in honoring God in all things, but that's what the spirit of religion does.

I want to spend a moment addressing something that we've become quite familiar with in ministering to a number of single young women who have been engaged as full-time missionaries in a foreign country.

Collectively they have all had a growing desire to get married, and have asked God to accommodate that desire. As the years have gone by and there has not only been no marriage, but there have been no suitors as well. That is supremely disappointing. We are all aware that a merry heart does good, (Proverbs 17:22) like a medicine, but hope deferred makes the heart sick. (Proverbs 13:12) For the most part these gals are mad at God because nothing positive has happened in that arena. In other words, they believe that they are suffering for Jesus.

The difficulty is that we humans tend to get stuck doing what we're doing, even if it's killing us. Whether it is believing that God hasn't changed his mind about you being a foreign missionary (simply because you haven't asked about it), or that He might tell you to take a lengthy sabbatical (didn't ask because you would feel unproductive), or that you think your season never changes and you wouldn't know what to do if it did.

Ladies and gentlemen, if this is your situation then you have raised more than one idol in your life that is keeping God at arm's length and binding Him from acting. I am not saying that there are not those who are to remain single all their lives, but God is not One who will require you to remain in a perpetual state of disappointment all your life. He will tell you are to remain celibate. If He hasn't, then that's not you. So be open to change.

What I am trying to say is that seasons in life do change. If I am still engaged in what I feel I have been called to and one of my chief unfulfilled desires is continuing to bring disappointment, then I have to go to God to find out if the season has changed and I am still hanging onto the old.

God can work miracles, but if you refuse to change your ways and engage other singles in the environment 'they' are in, what you are unconsciously doing is demanding that God work a miracle in your behalf. In the 40 years I have been pursuing the Lord I have never found Him to respond very well to the my demands.

It's rather like Joshua meeting that angelic representation of the Lord Jesus Christ who was carrying a sword. Joshua, only paying attention to the sword, demands to know, Are you friend or foe? Are you for us, or against us? The being responds with, *"Neither. I am the Commander of the army of the Lord."* (Joshua 5:13-15) Joshua immediately feel down and asked, What are we supposed to do? If you will not choose to embrace the possibility of change in order to achieve your dream, you might as well forget achieving it.

8

Tuning Your Receiver

If you want to see and hear in the spirit realm then you are going to have to intentionally turn on your spiritual ears and open your spiritual eyes. There is no other choice.

Over the years we have ministered to multitudes of folks who shut down, turned off, or dismissed some portion of themselves because they felt that it made them different, vulnerable, weird, strange or somehow alienated others with whom they wanted to be connected. Others did the same because they thought that characteristic made them open to be abused, taken advantage of, targeted, etc. In so doing they became something other than what they were created to be.

Let's spend a little time looking into what God had in mind that these folks never saw.

In Genesis 1:26, the Bible says that you and I were created in the image of God.

> Genesis 1:26-27 "*And God said, Let us make man in **our image, after our likeness**: and let them have dominion*

> *over the fish of the sea, and over the fowl of the air, and over the cattle, and over all the earth, and over every creeping thing that creepeth upon the earth. 27 So **God created man in his own image**, in the image of God created he him; male and female created he them."*

Then in John 4:24, Jesus said,

> "<u>God is a Spirit</u>: and they that worship him must worship in spirit and truth."

So since God is a spirit, and He created us in His image, were are primarily spirit beings.

In 1 Thessalonians 5:23 Paul says,

> "And the God of peace himself sanctify you wholly; and may **<u>your</u> <u>spirit and soul and body</u>** be preserved entire, without blame at the coming of our Lord Jesus Christ."

So what God has established for us is the fact that we were – and are – principally spirit beings. Which is why Paul says at the conclusion of his letters to the Galatians, Philippians, his second to Timothy, and from Philemon,

> "The grace of the Lord Jesus Christ be with <u>your spirit</u>."

According to 1 Thessalonians 5:23, there is an order to the way we are to live our lives;

1. our human spirit subjected to the spirit of God that dwells within us,
2. our human spirit ruling over our soul (defined as our mind, will and emotions),
3. which in turn is to rule over our body.

Here is the answer to, So What? According to the combined statement of Ephesians 1:3-4 and 2:10 above, the works that were prepared (determined) for us to perform before the foundation of the world are … spiritual works to be performed by …. spirit people using the …. spiritual blessings (gifts) He (God) has provided for us in Christ Jesus.

So what are the works?

First some background is needed. There was a war in heaven;

> Isaiah 14:12-14 " *How art thou fallen from heaven, O Lucifer, son of the morning! how art thou cut down to the ground, which didst weaken the nations! 13 For thou hast said in thine heart, I will ascend into heaven, I will exalt my throne above the stars of God: I will sit also upon the mount of the congregation, in the sides of the north: 14 I will ascend above the heights of the clouds; I will be like the most High. 15 Yet thou shalt be brought down to hell, to the sides of the pit."* (KJV)

So Lucifer was cast out of heaven to earth. Jesus, the faithful and true witness, declared in Luke 10:18, *"I beheld Satan as lightning fall from heaven."* (KJV)

Now there are two things that coincide here from these two passages. From Isaiah 12:14 we see the result of Lucifer's fall to the earth, *"which didst weaken the nations!"* Note the emphasis. It was very apparently to Isaiah when he had this vision that earth was a decidedly different place after Lucifer's banishment. Note also the words. The Hebrew word translated here as "weaken," is from a primitive root word meaning, "prostrate, overthrow, decay, waste away."

This state of continual decline is met by Jesus declaring to his disciples in Luke 10:19-20

> *"Behold, I give unto you power to tread on serpents and scorpions, and over all the power of the enemy: and nothing shall by any means hurt you. 20 Notwithstanding in this rejoice not, that the spirits are subject unto you; but rather rejoice, because your names are written in heaven."*

God is redemptive in all His ways. Therefore ... before there was a need for anything on this planet to be redeemed, there was ample provision ... 1 Peter 1:18-20 ... the lamb was slain for you and me before the foundation of the world. Before you sinned, there was the provision of forgiveness. Before you owed a debt you could not pay, there was provision. Before you needed a savior, there was a sacrifice.

So when Jesus said to His disciples, "I saw Lucifer bite the dust." And followed with ... Therefore,

> *"I give unto you power to tread on serpents and scorpions, and over all the power of the enemy: and nothing shall by any means hurt you."*

Jesus was establishing His right and His authority to redeem the earth and all its inhabitants. Since Jesus never saw demons as anything bigger than creepy crawly things, and satan was to be under His feet, He referred to them as scorpions and snakes. Harmful? Yes, but with the balm of Gilead, not deadly.

Why do I say not deadly? Because in Genesis 1:26, God created us in His image, his likeness. His word says he never sleeps nor slumbers, (Psalm 121) then neither does our human spirit. That is how David could say in Psalms 16 that his spirit (heart, same word in Hebrew) instructed him on his bed while he slept. At night my soul is in a temporary state of hibernation, while my body is being restored/re-invigorated/re-energized for the events of the coming day, but my spirit doesn't shut down. It can turn its face to the Lord and receive everything it needs for the coming day – if so inclined.

Further, since we are created in His image, and He is spirit, and He had no beginning, nor end, it is quite likely that our human spirits are eternal as well. To my mind, we have to be since he created us to dwell with Him forever in the hereafter of heaven.

To my mind, I think that concept is reinforced by Jeremiah 1:4-5,

> *"Then the word of the LORD came unto me, saying, 5 **Before** I formed you in the belly (womb) I knew you; and before you came forth out of the womb I sanctified you, and I ordained you as a prophet unto the nations."*

The Hebrew word in verse 5 translated as "knew" is the word 'yada.' It is the same word used when Adam "knew" Eve and she conceived a son.. It carries with it the inference that there is much more than just cognitive or even figurative knowledge of us as individuals, such as "I recognize you to be spirit # 4,578,692." It's so much more personal than that. To me it declares that we were first created as spirits and had a relationship with Him spirit-to-spirit prior to our appearance here on earth.

It also infers that He (God) created us for the purpose of some sort of intimate, interactive knowledge of us gained experientially. If that is true, then the hunger we have for God today is really in some way a desire to fulfill a distant memory of the ultimate connectedness we had before all the clutter and noise of this environment blocked it out.

Obviously, when we were created God desired mutual relationship such that we too knew God and would experience His character, goodness, etc, etc; that in this place in pre-history we would behold His beauty, His majesty, we would feel His love, and moment by moment commune with Him spirit to Spirit.

It is my belief that on that fateful day when God created us, He chose to build into us whatever was specifically needed to be effective in three arenas.

> Luke 12:32 *"Fear not, little flock; for it is your Father's good pleasure to give you the kingdom."*

Interestingly, elsewhere in the Word we are described as *"Ambassadors for Christ."* (2 Corinthians 5:20) We have become ambassadors of another Kingdom, and as such we have become the representatives of a superior Kingdom to this one and our job is to daily demonstrate the superiority of the Kingdom we represent to the subjects of the inferior kingdom we currently reside in. To that end, God had to pour into us some specific things that made us fit to be effective in the Kingdom of God.

> Philippians 2:13 *"For it is God which worketh in you both to will and to do of his good pleasure."*

At our creation God put into us whatever was require to insure that we would be responsive to Him in a manner that He could work in and through us. And ...

> Psalms 37:4 *"Delight thyself also in the LORD; and he shall give thee the desires of thine heart."*

Apparently there are specific desires that He has placed in our hearts which are connected to our identity and are coincident with our specific purpose.

Now I want to key on Jeremiah Chapter 1 because I believe that it is very important for us to understand the implications of it, both for ourselves and those to whom we minister. If you recall from Jeremiah 1:5 God declared that before Jeremiah had been placed in his mother's womb God had already determined that Jeremiah was going to be a prophet to the nations (destiny, calling, purpose) and God had sanctified him (set apart) for/unto that specific task.

I don't think this was an isolated incident applicable to Jeremiah only, but it is also applicable to each of us. Each of was created for a specific purpose and to fulfill a specific calling.

This is where Psalms 37:4 comes in. I believe that one day in Heaven there was a counsel held between the Father, Son and Holy Spirit. (That's kind of a weird thought since they are one.) They knew what Jeremiah was set to be, so they had to install some specific things in him in order for him to ever want to get close to doing it. So they had to install a specific mix of talents, abilities, intellect, personality, temperament, spiritual gifts, and inclinations, skills, etc., each of which was empowered by a hidden set of desires or driven-ness to be fulfilled. The total mix of all these ingredients I call "identity."

We are not told whether God told Jeremiah this when He was a young man, so he wouldn't stray off and try to become an engineer like somebody else I know, or much later on in his ministry as a confirmation when things got tough and he needed to be reminded that he was still in the center of God's will.

Here's one more scripture to consider;

> *Ephesians 2:10 'For we are his workmanship, created in Christ Jesus for good works, which God prepared beforehand, that we should walk in them."*

To me this verse is absolutely incontrovertible evidence that when God created you and me, we were created with a specific purpose in mind. Then when we throw in the next verse we see that all these individual purposes planned by God have been woven into a much bigger cosmic-sized tapestry to teach a specific group of entities the lesson of a life-time;

> *Ephesians 3:8-11 " To me (Paul), though I am the very least of all the saints, this grace was given, to preach to the Gentiles the unsearchable riches of Christ,*
> *9 and to bring to light for everyone what is the plan of the mystery hidden for ages in God who created all things,*
> *10 so that **through the church** the manifold wisdom of God might now be made known **to the rulers and authorities in the heavenly places.***
> *11 This was according to the **eternal purpose** that he has realized in Christ Jesus our Lord,"*

We cannot blithely skip over the fact that all these interwoven individual purposes were created to be an integral part of this larger strategic strategy which was also created before the foundation of the world – an eternal purpose.

This is why I feel that we are born with an internal cry to connect with God. However, because we are in the domain of the *"prince of the power of the air"* who caused a veil to close between us and The One who sent us, all those personal intimate communication means were cut off. When we entered the womb of our mother we didn't have a developed brain in which to store them, so all the memories of those bygone days evaporated. Just a hint of them remain; somewhat like the faint smell of home cooking in the evening air; we can't quite identify what it actually is, but the slightly familiar aroma tells us via the fragments of the memory that something good is on the stove.

The transfer of duty stations also cut us off from the all consuming love of God we used to continually experience, and we have tried as hard as we can to replace it with whatever we could grab hold of. We come into this world expecting to be recognized, appreciated, and valued just like it was in our previous abode, but we're in a different time zone; we have a foreign zip code; and can't seem to make it happen.

It is that same special "identity" mix He installed in you that makes you uniquely you. It was the Father's delight to make only one of "you," because only you, with that unique collection of expressions of gifts, talents, acquired skills, wants, personality, dreams and desires could perform that pre-determined set of *"good works"* (Ephesians 2:10) that He created you to perform before the foundation of the world.

Now Jesus said something rather interesting in Matthew 16:18 *"... I will build my church ..."* Catholics have so overemphasized the phrase that immediately precedes this one that the latter gets completely lost. Jesus said, "I" not Peter, not Billy Graham, not anyone else you can name either, although each of these has made his or her contribution. What you must understand is that each of us has a specific contribution to make, which when connected to all the other individual contributions builds something that only Christ Himself could have accomplished.

For some, their contribution is business. Not only earning money but building people in the process; changing one element of our culture by their investment in those who work for them. That is one of the reasons why I chose to co-write the book *Choose Your Outcome* with Mandy Valdes. (Available on Amazon.com) Mandy's view of a business owner's responsibility is to reshape the family destiny of each of his employees, who are largely young high school kids from dysfunctional family units, so that what they are currently experiencing is not replicated in the next generation. He is not only one of the wisest men I know, but his personal ministry in and through the business demonstrates his heart for those who are struggling to make a better life for themselves.

After the rough and rocky start of a barbeque restaurant in Campbellsville, KY, Josh Tucker, the founder and owner of Brothers BBQ, came to the conclusion that he was really in business for the people, almost exclusively for his employees. His actual job was to grow them and build into their lives all he could during their time with him, the fact that their lives had meaning and were important to him and to the world. Since he came to that revelation his business has tripled.

For some it's medicine, media, mental health, law enforcement, education, civil service; changing one element of our culture by their investment in those who work with and for them, as well as for whom they work.

These are not people operating Christian businesses; they are Christians doing things that build the Kingdom one day at a time, doing what only they were created to do.

I am going to jump up on my soapbox for a minute and tell all those who poo-poo the Seven Mountain Strategy created in 1975 by Bill Bright (founder of Campus Crusade for Christ) and Loren Cunningham (founder of Youth With A Mission YWAM), and lately publicized by Lance Walnau, to wake up and get a life.

Both men (Bright & Cunningham) had been given a dream by God, containing a message to give to the other. That message was about the Seven Mountains of influence in our culture. Francis Schaeffer received a similar message from the Lord at about the same time. All three believed that in order for the church to impact the world for Jesus Christ and fulfill the commands of Matthew 28, it would be necessary for elements of the church to influence the Seven Mountains of influence in our society. "The Mountains" being the major core spheres of influence in any society; Family, Religion/Faith, Education, Government/Law, Media/News, Arts/Entertainment and Business/Economics.

In Matthew 28 Jesus gave His disciples some very specific directions that also apply to you and I, and our alternate interpretation of what He said will not be greeted well on Judgment Day.

> *Matthew 28:18-20 "And Jesus came and said to them, "All authority in heaven and on earth has been given to me.*

> *19 Go therefore and **make disciples of all nations**, baptizing them in the name of the Father and of the Son and of the Holy Spirit,*
> *20 **teaching them** to observe all that I have commanded you. And behold, I am with you always, to the end of the age."*

I am very familiar with numerous ministries that are doing great things all over the world from the prospective of evangelism. They are winning thousands to the Lord and in their zeal for salvations are then moving on to greener pastures. A few of these ministries have followed up to the degree that they have thought to establish churches in these rural communities by appointing one of the new converts as its pastor. In most cases in Africa it has fallen to one who cannot read, or one who is a converted witch doctor, so the gospel of Jesus Christ gets mixed with all manner of local superstition and tribal beliefs.

Obviously, the discipleship of an entire nation is a task greater than any one person can tackle. There must be multiple, even multiplied thousands of individuals involved in the task on a daily basis. The task is to bring a level of influence to bear upon each individual element of society such that it brings its operational policy, procedures and philosophy into alignment with the King of Kings.

This can only be accomplished if there are those, who were created by the foreknowledge of God with those specific desires, skills and motivations (purposes), who will move into those areas and exert their influence to make the changes possible, and through those positions of influence disciple that area of the culture.

If your children are not raised with the idea that they and the others of their generation were created for this task they will not consider this to be part of their preferred future or sacred obligation. They will do what they want to do without ever understanding that what they do plays a vital role in a much bigger play. The lack of understanding of it also means lack of cooperation with it,

So for those of you who have thrown out the idea of the Seven Mountain initiative as putting undue pressure on parents and children to raise mind molders, world shapers and history makers, you have to understand that they will naturally influence their environment positively or negatively with or without your instruction. You have an obligation to positively influence their views from which you cannot escape.

For those of you who still cling to the idea that the Seven Mountain thing is little more than another form of dominion theology promulgated by a bunch of obscure college whackos that includes a mandate for Christians to control civil affairs and all other aspects of society in order for Christ to return, you have missed to whole point of the message of Matthew 28. You have gotten so wrapped up in looking at the words that you have totally missed the message.

The point of Matthew 28 isn't about control, it is about influence. Evil is alive and well in this world and all the elements of its culture are in control. We were all created to be effective in various areas of our culture and our individual job is to be the Ambassador for Christ, reconciling all those who are estranged from Him to Him. As we do our job we will naturally want to teach them what Holy Spirit has brought to us (John 14:26) that has changed the way we live.

Discipleship is not about dominion or control, it is a spiritual work (exercise) that produces a spiritual transaction which sets us free to love and reap the fullness of relationship that God intended – real life.

So what does all this mean?

This means you are going to have to identify and begin to train and efficiently operate in your spiritual gifts.

Now if you were brought up as I was in one of the primary mainline denominational churches the definition of spiritual gifts exclusively served the institutional church's needs; hospitality, gifts of service (cleaning the building, etc), teaching a Sunday school class, serving in the nursery, et, etc. etc. I am not saying that these things are not a good idea and aren't necessary in the community you are a part of, but if this is all that spiritual gifts mean then you have consumed waaay too much of the cool aide.

Now get this!!! The Institutional church is NOT the Kingdom! It may be one tiny expression of it, but IT IS NOT the Kingdom of God. Anyone who says differently has an agenda you don't want to be a part of. Anyone can help, anyone can serve, it's just part of being in the club and you don't even have to have a relationship with God to do that. So if that's been your definition of spiritual gifts, you gotta throw that overboard and get a new set.

Your spiritual gifts are part of what God sowed into you when He created you and they are to be one of the expressions of purpose for which you were created;

> *1Corinthians 12:6 -11 "And there are diversities of operations, but it is the same God which worketh all in all.*
> *7 But the manifestation of the Spirit is given to every man to profit withal.*
> *8 For to one is given by the Spirit the **word of wisdom**; to another the **word** of knowledge by the same Spirit;*
> *9 To another **faith** by the same Spirit; to another the gifts of **healing** by the same Spirit;*
> *10 To another the working of **miracles**; to another **prophecy**; to another **discerning of spirits**; to another divers kinds of **tongues**; to another the interpretation of tongues:*
> *11 But all these worketh (by) that one and the selfsame Spirit, dividing to every man severally as he will." (KJV)*

I have searched and searched, but to the best of my ability I could not find the spiritual gift of parking lot attendant, nursery worker, usher, communion juice preparer, offering counters, sound board operator or attendance takers listed anywhere. It may be in another translation, but it wasn't in any of them that I could find. So if this is how you have defined yourself as serving the Lord, you need to take another look at this whole passage and your life, because something significant is missing. This sounds more like a club.

Next, you are going to have to begin to interface with the world through your human spirit rather than through your mind and your five senses. When you read your Bible you are going to have to start looking for the difference between a Capital S (Holy Spirit) and a lower case s (human spirit), otherwise you're going to miss your instructions big time.

> *Matthew 22:43 "He saith unto them, How then doth David in spirit call him Lord, saying,"*

Matthew 26:41 *"Watch and pray, that ye enter not into temptation: the spirit indeed is willing, but the flesh is weak."*

Luke 1:47 *"And my spirit hath rejoiced in God my Saviour."*

Luke 8:55 *"And her spirit came again, and she arose straightway: and he commanded to give her meat."*

John 4:24 *"God is a Spirit: and they that worship him must worship him in spirit and in truth.*

John 6:63 *"It is the spirit that quickeneth; the flesh profiteth nothing: the words that I speak unto you, they are spirit, and they are life."*

Galatians 6:18 *"Brethren, the grace of our Lord Jesus Christ be with your spirit. Amen."*

2Timothy 4:22 *"The Lord Jesus Christ be with thy spirit. Grace be with you. Amen."* (KJV)

<u>Philemon 1:25</u> *"The grace of our Lord Jesus Christ be with your spirit. Amen."*

When King David said in Psalms 42:5;

"Why art thou cast down, O my soul? and why art thou disquieted in me? hope thou in God: for I shall yet praise him for the help of his countenance."

What portion of him was speaking to his soul? It was his spirit calling his soul to a higher place, a place of hope and trust in the Lord, not one of disappointment and depression because things didn't seem to work out like expected.

All these scriptures point to the fact that the Lord is very interested in you learning to walk out life through your human spirit, not your head. That's how He created you. But when you accepted the Lord Jesus Christ as your savior, you got a bonus. You has His precious Holy Spirit come take up residence in the only place in your being that speaks the same language – your human spirit. So you have access to everything you need for life and Godliness, you have the mind of Christ dwelling there, and you have need of no other teacher, if you'll listen to him.

Next, you are going to have to begin hearing the voice of the Holy Spirit within you and being obedient to it.

> John 5:25 *"Verily, verily, I say unto you, The hour is coming, and now is, when the dead shall hear the voice of the Son of God: and they that hear shall live."*
>
> John 5:28 *"Marvel not at this: for the hour is coming, in the which all that are in the graves shall hear his voice",*
>
> John 10:3 *"To him the porter openeth; and the sheep hear his voice: and he calleth his own sheep by name, and leadeth them out."*
>
> John 10:4 *"And when he putteth forth his own sheep, he goeth before them, and the sheep follow him: for they know his voice."*
>
> John 10:5 *"And a stranger will they not follow, but will flee from him: for they know not the voice of strangers."*
>
> John 10:16 *"And other sheep I have, which are not of this fold: them also I must bring, and they shall hear my voice; and there shall be one fold, and one shepherd.*

> John 10:27 *"My sheep hear my voice, and I know them, and they follow me:"* That was Jesus speaking by the way.

In fact, there are three (3) voices that you should be able to hear and distinguish between; the voice of the Lord (or Holy Spirit), your voice (the self talk you are used to hearing, usually negative) and the voice of the enemy (probably the one you are most used to hearing but couldn't differentiate it from your own.)

You cannot do these things without engaging the spirit realm with your human spirit. Unfortunately, you've probably been warned about doing so by some well meaning (albeit ignorant) pastor who sold you on the dangers of messing around with New Age stuff. The reality of the spirit realm is this ... Who created it? Lucifer sure as heck didn't, so that only leaves One guy.

If God created it, then Jesus used it – to his advantage and apparently taught His disciples how to use it. Here are some examples;

- Thomas was instantly bodily transported (translated) in the spirit from Gaza to Azotus after traveling from Jerusalem to Gaza to lead an Ethiopian to the Lord and baptizing him. Acts 8:26-40
- Paul spends time in heaven. Revelation 1:10
- Jesus recounts a conversation between Lazarus (a beggar) and Abraham across the divide between hell and heaven (purgatory?). Luke 16:21-30
- Jesus walks through a crowd in the temple intent on stoning him. John 8:59

- Jesus appears to His disciples then vanishes. Luke 24:31
- Enoch does not die but is translated directly into heaven. Hebrews 11:5
- Jesus transports a boat and his disciples (boat and all) from the middle of the Sea of Galilee to the shore instantly, after walking half way across the lake to greet them. John 6:21
- Jesus is surround by Jews intent on killing him in the temple – He disappears ... again. John 10:39
- Jesus disappears from his disciples. John 12:36
- Jesus walks into another dimension and is transfigured appearing with Elijah and Moses, Mark 9:2-4
- Elijah does not die but is picked up and escorted into heaven by a chariot driven by an angel. 2Kings 2
- Joshua cannot finish a battle and asks for the sun not to go down until he's finished. It does.

Notice that I didn't include healings, miracles, and other extraordinary things that Jesus, His disciples and other followers of God accomplished. These events highlight the thinness of the veil between this realm, where things are somewhat limited, and the realm of the spirit, where anything is possible. Further, it says those capabilities and capacities in the spirit realm are useful for operating in this realm, and are even endorsed by Jesus and His disciples.

Let me ask you a question, and you'll have to put on your spiritual thinking cap to answer this one ... What did Jesus know about how spirit stuff working in this realm that enabled Him to do the things He did?

You have to understand that God did not have the Bible written exclusively to recount the deeds of Jesus, although that was the vast majority of His reasoning. There is another element of truth that God is trying to convey through these stories;

If you walk in the power and knowledge of the spirit realm while in God directed pursuits anything is possible.

The appearance of a single story in the Bible is not only intended to document a specific event, but to announce its potential for all of us to engage in the very same thing that was described in that account.

The appearance of a single story in the Bible is not only intended to document that event, but to stir your curiosity about spiritual things so that you'll begin to open your spirit eyes and spirit ears to see, hear, understand and potentially do them.

Before you write this off as BS, consider the full implications of these two passages;

> *2Corinthians 5:17-20 "Therefore if any man be in Christ, he is a new creature: old things are passed away; behold, all things are become new.*
> *18 And all things are of God, who hath reconciled us to himself by Jesus Christ, and hath given to us the ministry of reconciliation;*
> *19 To wit, that God was in Christ, reconciling the world unto himself, not imputing their trespasses unto them; and hath committed unto us the word of reconciliation.*
> *20 Now then we are ambassadors for Christ,"*

What does it mean to be an ambassador? An ambassador is a credentialed citizen of another country (realm) sent under the authority of the sovereign of that land to demonstrate, by various means, the superiority of its rules, regulations, way of life and commerce of that land or Kingdom to the authorities and citizens of an inferior kingdom.

Lucifer was booted out of heaven. It is no longer his domain. He has no authority there. He was banished to earth. This is his domain and he has authority here. But he still retains his 'spiritual' form, knowledge and identity, which he has used against us for his benefit.

The sole reason things have not gone well for we humans here on earth is that we have forgotten where we came from, what Kingdom we are actually citizens of, the power of the ruler of that Kingdom (even in this foreign land) and we have never chosen to learn the rules, regulations, ways of life and commerce of our real homeland. So it's little wonder that no one can tell the difference between Christians and any other inhabitant of this realm.

Let's go back to the stories in the book of John where Jesus is totally surrounded in the temple by people who were dead set on killing him. First thing to recall is that the buildings, and specifically the Jewish temples, of the 1st Century AD were not as large structures as the structures we have today. Local construction materials did not allow them to create venues where more than a couple of hundred people could congregate at one time. So when the Bible says he was surrounded, it means that it was probably standing room only, side to side, shoulder to shoulder, kind of conditions.

Secondly, the men who surrounded him were angry and violent with rage that someone would come into their midst and tell them that they had it all wrong, as did their forefathers, and further that their prized leaders were a bunch of vultures preying upon them.

Back in this day there was no leniency for first offenders, no political correctness, no instant forgiveness for someone with a different viewpoint. It was death by stoning and anyone could and would participate, and furthermore, it was seen as their civic and religious duty to permanently stamp out dissenting opinion that clashed with the status quo. There was no half heartedness in their desire to see Jesus lying dead in the dust with his head bashed in – it was their sacred duty.

So how did he escape their clutches?

Theoretical physicists have been searching for decades to find what they have described as the "God Equation." The God Equation is presumed to be a single or interconnected series of mathematical expressions that takes into account every other existing equation proven by experiment and observation; such as gravitational pull, those governing energy state transformation, star formation and extinction, radiation production of various wavelengths, accounts for black holes, those which govern the characteristics of light, sound, motion, conservation of energy and energy conversion, etc. Whether such an equation actually exists or not is a mute point because these physicists have observed such an order for all these various phenomenon there must be an over-arching expression which coordinates and accommodates them all.

What they have surmised thus far is that they have found a set of conditions that will indeed allow this if there are a sufficient number of dimensions available. Some have expressed them as folds in time and space through which one could step into or out of the current reality into a past or future reality – in the same place. That possible number of dimensions has been whittled down in recent years to either 11, 13, 27 or 29.

What this tells us is this. If we can figure out how to move from this dimension to another and back again, we can travel to any time, space, or place possible. This obviously has spawned a number of SYFY movie plots (such as the Terminator franchise) where someone with special knowledge from the future comes back in time to save humanity from future extinction.

Back to our story of Jesus being completely surrounded by an angry, blood-thirsty mob of zealots hell-bent on his destruction, and somehow he escapes – simply disappears. Not only does he do this once, but multiple times in various environments. What did he know about the construction of the universe that allowed him to move inter-dimensionally at will and walk away without a scratch?

Most folks would simply shrug it off as, "Well. He's Jesus. He's actually God in a man-suit. He can do anything he wants." Then they expect you to be satisfied with that non-answer. Their glib response disqualifies their answer. Because Jesus was wearing a "man-suit," being fully man and fully God says that he chose to limit himself to what mortal men would be limited to. After all, he had to eat, drink, sleep, and clothe himself just like we do. But because He was God, we can assume that He had not completely left behind, nor totally invalidated His heavenly knowledge of how things were created to function into order to fulfill His mission in life. Since He created all things (John 1), we might consider that He knew a few things we don't.

What is my point?

What I am trying to get you to see is that unless you intentionally choose to open your spiritual eyes and open your spiritual ears none of these options will ever be open, or available to you when you need them or when the Father asks you to. Jesus said, He could do nothing in His home town because of their unbelief. Keeping your spiritual senses dulled eradicates your ability to believe what God could do in your circumstances and thereby disqualifies it from happening for you when you desperately need it.

For some, these kind of questions are off limits because they consider them to be new age spiritism and even part of occult teaching that will lead you into a spiritual ditch. That which does not lead you to God will lead you to fear. Jesus said that *you were not given a spirit of fear, but one of love, power and a sound mind.* (1 Timothy 1:7)

In the last few decades we have documented in numerous books the experiences of many people who in dreams found themselves traveling to various Muslim countries to teach Bible studies or preach to small groups of men or women gathered in homes. I know six of them myself. My wife is one of them. The interesting thing is that when they return and tell of the experiences to someone who has actually lived in the country, the description of the pattern and construction of dishes, cookware, rugs and furniture is highly accurate, when none of them had ever been there. How do you know these facts without having detailed prior knowledge of everyday life in the Middle East? Answer: You had to be there.

I want to re-emphasize this point once more; single events in the Bible are so much more than the recounting of a single event. Consider the following that we have already discussed which is found in Jeremiah 1:4-5

> *"4 Then the word of the LORD came unto me, saying, 5 Before I formed thee in the belly I knew thee; and before*

> *thou camest forth out of the womb I sanctified thee, and I ordained thee a prophet unto the nations."*

Essentially the Bible is pointing out that you and I were similarly created; He sanctified (set us apart) us and ordained us to do specific things. The only thing different is that God told him very early in life. I think God is speaking these things to us, but we have neither chosen to hear, nor see what He was trying to get us to engage.

Now consider this; There is NO such word as failure in the vocabulary of the Kingdom. The Old Testament says,

> Psalms 37:23 *"The steps of a good man are ordered by the LORD: and he delighteth in his way. 24 Though he fall, he shall not be utterly cast down: for the LORD upholdeth him with his hand."*

> Proverbs 24:16 *"For a just man falleth seven times, and riseth up again: but the wicked shall fall into mischief."*

Then in the New Testament Jesus takes this principle to a whole new level when he speaks to Peter about the failures of another man,

> Matthew 18:21-22 *"Then came Peter to him, and said, Lord, how oft shall my brother sin against me, and I forgive him? till seven times? 22 Jesus saith unto him, I say not unto thee, Until seven times: but, Until seventy times seven."*

As you can plainly see from this single example, the principles and ways of the Kingdom are decidedly different than what the system of this world has taught us. We need to intentionally identify them and systematically un-learn them, then intentionally begin to walk in the ways of God. See Psalm 139:23 and 24.

If we were to eliminate this Word from our vocabulary as well, it would change our whole perspective of how we engage with other people at home, in our work environment and on the street or market place. There would be no need to "straighten them out" because of our judgment on what they do as being a failure, but would cause us to encourage them to live life in a manner more helpful and healthful for them. In other words, being a blessing rather than one who curses.

I have repeated this for you because I want it to help you change the way you engage with the Word of God. The Bible is the written instruction about how the Kingdom currently works, not just a collection of stories about how things went. So we need to begin to read it with spiritual eyes so that the whole meaning doesn't pass by us undetected and totally un-appreciated. Without that understanding you will never be able to make the connection to the Kingdom of God that Jesus wants you to have. That's why there are so many stories about the things he did. Each one reveals another element of the Kingdom. In them there is life, which is the fundamental reason He came to earth in human form.

Remember this ... because this is really what it is all about as you do whatever it is you do on a daily basis ...

> Mark 16:15-20 "And he said unto them, Go ye into all the world, and preach the gospel to every creature.
> **16 He that believeth and is baptized shall be saved;**

*17 And **these signs shall follow them that believe;** In my name shall they cast out devils; they shall speak with new tongues;*
18 They shall take up serpents; and if they drink any deadly thing, it shall not hurt them; they shall lay hands on the sick, and they shall recover.
19 So then after the Lord had spoken unto them, he was received up into heaven, and sat on the right hand of God.
*20 And they went forth, and preached everywhere, **the Lord working with them, and confirming the word with signs following**. Amen." (KJV)*

You and are supposed to be working miracles large and small while in the midst of going about our normal activities.

1John 4:17b *"because as he is, so are we in this world."*

9

Following the deaths of a number of young black men at the hands of police in the last 24 months, much has been made of the slogan "Black Lives Matter." It has been followed by other slogans, including "Blue Lives Matter" following the senseless murder of polices officers as they were pumping gas into their patrol car or gunned down on the street.

The most recent voice was one decrying the violence on both sides; "All Lives Matter." As I was pondering this latest addition to the sloganeering, I saw this one from two opposing sides, each having significant implications for all of us.

The first is that indeed, to God All Lives Matter. He created each one with a purpose, and if I do say so, a redemptive purpose. Some might argue this is not so by citing the verses in Romans 9:21-22

> "Hath not the potter power over the clay, of the same lump to make one vessel unto honor, and another unto dishonor? What if God, willing to show his wrath, and to make his power known, endured with much longsuffering the vessels of wrath fitted to destruction: "

This supposedly declares that some were created for evil purposes so God could show His power by crushing them. To that I'd say you've missed the point of the rest of the book completely. If this was indeed the heart of God, why then would He show such patience toward evil doers if not for a desire on His part to see them change before His judgment fell?

It really boils down to personal choice. I have been around multiple siblings who were all products of the same dysfunctional, abusive parents where most chose to walk the high road, unlike that of their parents, and only one chose the dark side and became worse that their parents. It's all personal choice. God made us all with redeeming value. It's our choice what we exhibit.

The world is full of malcontents who believe that they've gotten a raw deal and somebody owes them something. Their anger colors every decision they make and most of them are bad. Until there is a change of heart their decisions will always be bad because there will never be enough retribution to satisfy them. If that is your posture, then to you no life matters.

The second point of my pondering led me to this;

All lives don't necessarily matter; Seemingly only the Ones who make their lives matter do.

If the only thing you can do with your life is to hate, be miserable and demand justice (ie, have someone do what you think is right for you) then your life will never matter to anyone else, except maybe your momma. Your life only matters if you are serving someone else; making their world a little better place, solving a problem by bringing meaningful solutions, not standing on some street corner constantly bitching about stuff!

My wife and I are former tennis players and are consequently tennis fans. If you were able to watch the Women's finals of the 2018 US Open Tennis tournament you saw Serina Williams emotionally explode all over the court after having received a warning from the chair umpire, then being docked a point for being "coached" during the match.

Admittedly, women's tennis is officiated differently and that needs to be addressed, in spite of the fact that her coach did indeed admit to coaching her during the match, in which she was getting her butt kicked. However, her explosion escalated into demanding an apology from the umpire, calling him a thief for stealing a point from her and declaring that he will never chair another match she was in as long as he lived. For that tirade, she was docked a full game.

The thing that irked me and hundreds of thousands of other tennis fans was during her post-game interview she claimed that she had to do it because she was fighting for women's rights and all mothers, when most everyone knew the real problem was that since she was a former champion, and a new mom, that she felt that she should receive deferential treatment and be allowed to engage her coach (while in the match, even though it is against the rules) since she was getting beaten so badly.

This is at the heart of the political chaos we are experiencing in the US right now. One group was disappointed that they didn't get what they wanted so they have to do whatever they can to see to it that the other groups gets nothing out of it either. Consequently, our Congress hasn't done one thing for the nation in three years. We all suffer now.

As my wife and I walked down a street in Asheville, NC recently and she noticed a bumper sticker that said, "If you can't hug a tree, stop breathing their air." I understand what he or she was trying to say, but the attitude of violence in the statement discounted the entire message. No lives matter if you can't think like me! The net result of this level of "caring" for the environment is to do nothing but make a brash statement, which revealed how insensitive this person actually is toward the remainder of living things. Caring is doing, not talking about other people doing or not doing.

Folks, the promise that God made to Abram in Genesis 12:2 was that he was blessed by God to "be a blessing." That declaration is the same for you and I, you are blessed by God (in the manner and with the specificity of how He created you) to be a blessing to the balance of creation. Why else would he have said, in

> Romans 8:19 *"For the creation waits with eager longing for the revealing of the sons of God."*

That's you and me folks – the ones who have made their lives count for the Kingdom of Heaven, not the dark side. That's the folks whose lives matter.

Speaking of being a blessing … Kentucky is the home of Bourbon production and some of the best corn ever produced goes into making bourbon. The story goes that there was a local farmer who grew excellent quality corn which he sold each year at a premium price to distillers. Every year he won the award for the best grown corn. One year a newspaper reporter interviewed him and learned something very interesting about how this man grew his corn. The reporter learned that every year this farmer shared his seed corn with his neighbors. "How can you afford to share your high production seed corn with your neighbors when each of them is competing directly with you every year?" the reporter asked.

"Well sir," replied the farmer, "the winds picks up pollen from my ripening corn and shares it with my neighbors. The pollen from my neighbor's ripening corn does the same for mine. If my neighbors grow inferior corn every year, my corn crop will steadily degrade every year. If I am going to grow good corn I have to help my neighbors grow good corn as well."

So it is with our lives. If we want to live meaningful lives (that matter) we must help enrich the lives of others as well.

Here's another somewhat more philosophic viewpoint, written by an economist, that follows upon the heels of, and supports the previous point; **Adam Smith** in his 1776 book "*An Inquiry into the Nature and Causes of the Wealth of Nations*" identified a significant Kingdom principle, and in so doing, coined a term he called "the invisible hand" (which has some obvious implications for believers).

In his book he states: "*Every individual necessarily labours to render the annual revenue of the society as great as he can. He generally neither intends to promote the public interest, nor knows how much he is promoting it ... He intends only his own gain, and he is in this, as in many other cases, led by an invisible hand to promote an end which was no part of his intention. Nor is it always the worse for society that it was no part of his intention. By pursuing his own interest he frequently promotes that of the society more effectually than when he really intends to promote it.*"

Thus, the "invisible hand" is essentially a natural (I think Godly supernatural principle) phenomenon that guides **free markets** and **capitalism** through competition for scarce resources for the benefit of all.

Do not misunderstand me – if you are in that season of life where raising children takes all the energy you have, or earning a living to support your family takes all your time and energy, you are doing what you are supposed to do. Your life matters as you teach them to be a blessing to others. The "invisible hand" will help them become a blessing to others as well.

10

The Great Cosmic War

Now, with all of the previous things being said about the uniqueness of your creation to achieve a specific purpose, it is also my guess that there was another party there that was a witnessed to all of God's magnificent creative display the day you and I were made ... Lucifer. He was probably there applauding each and every exquisite choice The Father made as He lovingly fashioned you for His purposes, silently taking note of everything Father did.

Sometime later, Lucifer began to think that he should at the least be on the same level as, or perhaps even *higher, than God* ...

> *Ezekiel 28:14-17 "Thou art the anointed cherub that covereth; and I have set thee so: thou wast upon the holy mountain of God; thou hast walked up and down in the midst of the stones of fire.*
> *15 Thou wast perfect in thy ways from the day that thou wast created, till iniquity was found in thee.*
> *16 By the multitude of thy merchandise they have filled the midst of thee with violence, and thou hast sinned: therefore I will cast thee as profane out of the mountain*

> *of God: and I will destroy thee, O covering cherub, from the midst of the stones of fire.*
> *17 Thine heart was lifted up because of thy beauty, thou hast corrupted thy wisdom by reason of thy brightness: I will cast thee to the ground, I will lay thee before kings, that they may behold thee."*

... and there was a war in Heaven. Lucifer's lost, and the sentence for his thoughts and actions was pronounced by God;

> *Ezekiel 28:18 "You have defiled thy sanctuaries by the multitude of thine iniquities, by the iniquity of thy traffic; therefore will I bring forth a fire from the midst of thee, it shall devour thee, and I will bring thee to ashes upon the earth in the sight of all them that behold thee. 19 All they that know thee among the people shall be astonished at thee: thou shalt be a terror, and never shall thou be any more."*

So Lucifer got his butt kicked, and he and his whole rebellious crew were booted out of Heaven: *"And he (Jesus) said unto them, I beheld satan as lightning fall from heaven."* (Luke 10:18)

> *Revelations 12:7-9 "And there was war in heaven: Michael and his angels fought against the dragon; and the dragon fought and his angels, 8 And prevailed not; neither was their place found any more in heaven. 9 And the great dragon was cast out, that old serpent, called the Devil, and Satan, which deceiveth the whole world: he was cast out into the earth, and his angels were cast out with him."*

> Isaiah 14:12-14 *"How art thou fallen from heaven, O Lucifer, son of the morning! how art thou cut down to the ground, which didst weaken the nations! 13 For thou*

> *hast said in thine heart, I will ascend into heaven, I will exalt my throne above the stars of God: I will sit also upon the mount of the congregation, in the sides of the north: 14 I will ascend above the heights of the clouds; I will be like the most High."*

I think it is interesting to note that our God is always merciful, even as he was merciful to Lucifer by not obliterating him as an entity from the universe when he decided He wanted to become the boss of everything. God knows, there are many of us who from time to time would love to have that job ourselves if we could.

Unfortunately for us, God didn't annihilate him, so his high impact face plant destination was the earth where he became known as:

> *"Wherein in time past ye walked according to the course of this world, according to the* **prince of the power of the air***, the spirit that now worketh in the children of disobedience." (Ephesians 2:2).*

The war between he (now known as the devil or satan) and God continues to this day..

Once Lucifer was "shown the door," make that, "given the left foot of fellowship," and found himself doing a serious face-plant on planet earth, he was really mad! Mad at God, mad at where he found himself, mad at his demotion, mad at what he saw when he arrived (dinosaurs and the like) and eventually mad at man when he showed up! As the new king of this domain he immediately set about to try to show God a thing or two about His prized possessions, His creation and the people He fashioned for Himself for "His good pleasure!"

That is how you and I came to be involved in this overarching cosmic war between God and satan.

So he (the devil, satan, the former Lucifer) tricked Adam and Eve, the first man and woman sent to earth to rectify (redeem) the damage (John 10:10) that Lucifer had done when he was sentenced to earth, turning it over to him authority over the earth that he received in Genesis 1:26-28. Through that broken and sinful pair, God established a race of people to call His own and through them brought the 2nd Adam (Jesus), the first a natural son, the second a spiritual son to redeem both earth and man. (1 Corinthians 15:46)

(So, our charter is essentially the same as that given to the original Adam, except that we now have the power of the Holy Spirit within us to help get it done.)

In his wrath satan knew how each of us was created and probably what we were created for because he was one of the original witnesses to our creation.

(Sometimes you can tell a great deal about a person's destiny by simply identifying where and how they have been attacked over their lifetime.) So that was what he went after – our personal identity and purpose. If you don't know who you are and why you are here, everything's an option for you. That's similar to the old saying, *"If you don't know where you're going, any road will take you there."* Most of us know the pain of winding up in a place we had no business being, and the arduous task of getting back on course.

So satan's attack is launched against who you are – your identity. He doesn't need to assign a horde of demons to your case to keep you messed you up. He started with your ancestors getting them to fall into all sorts of sin and entanglements. They built numerous mental ideologies and structures of thoughts about why things are the way they are (called their truth) and why stuff happens. They dutifully taught them to their children, so in time they eventually became your truth as well, even if it had no resemblance to the real truth and reality of life at all. These things are called iniquitous family patterns and belief systems; things like how you treat women or children; how you think about other races; thought process about poverty and material possessions. These things get passed on from generation to generation.

Their behavior also brought on curses and demonic attachments. The curses were reinforced by each successive generation and the demonic attachments grew stronger as each generation fell into the same sin as their predecessors.

Then there were the direct assaults against your personhood, when you were at your weakest and most vulnerable. These included vicious wounds like the death of a parent(s), divorce, abandonment, sexual molestation, rape, sodomy, rejection, poverty, mental and physical abuse, emotional and physical abandonment, or having had to grow up with parents who were drug or alcohol addicted, or who were rage-aholics.

In response to the pain of each event you built walls out of fear of experiencing further hurt and pain. They in turn kept out everything, including the love you so desperately desired; more trauma occurred and the enemy was there to feed you more lies about yourself.

For so many it meant living a life completely numb, with no highs or lows, because significant portions of your heart were shut down to the potential of more pain years ago. Simply existing is no fun whatsoever for there is no 'real' life there. After a few years it's hard to even say that it is better than what you had. Yes, there's no daily or weekly pain, but there's no joy either. The best you can say is that at least it's predictable.

Over time you find yourself in a place of isolation and disconnection, with a heart that is shut down and cold as a stone. You may yearn for real life, but everything seems to be a poor imitation. The enemy has you right where he wants you. You've lost touch with who you are, or you've failed to develop your own identity because the real you has been in hiding for most of your life. Since you have no clue who you really are, and have no idea why you're here, there is no corresponding sense of destiny, or purpose. Hence there is no vision, no passion and no opportunity for fulfillment.

We have all been there on one level or another. To those who have been horrifically abused and traumatized, is feels like a lifetime and there appears to be no hope for a come-back.

Then there are the spiritual attacks against our Spiritual and relational progress. The enemy doesn't like it at all when you are beginning to mature and do things like forgiving offences and determining not to judge each other, growing close with other believers and spending time with family. Nor can he allow you to accidentally get close to following your dreams. John 10:10a says,

> *"The thief cometh not, but for to steal, and to kill, and to destroy:"*

which is another way of saying,

> *"...In the world ye shall have tribulation:"* (John 16:33)

But there's good news. Jesus said in,

> John 10:10b *"I am come that they might have life, and that they might have it more abundantly."*

When Jesus appeared on the scene, in whom was all the fullness of God Himself, He firmly established the fact that there was a new Sheriff in town! He went about deputizing (giving authority to) all who would follow him. To those Deputies He gave the 'dunamis' power of the Holy Spirit to kick spiritual butt and take names; to break the power of sin (generational and otherwise) off man, to break the power of the defilement of sin off the land and set it free to be a blessing to man, and to re-establish Kingdom order in the house!

Now you know why the enemy's after your personal identity.

The good news is … as hard as this seems to be on us, God has a plan and He's not concerned about achieving His heart's purposes at all. He has secretly been preparing a mighty army of folks who have been through hell and have survived to help others. These folks may or may not be in a church. Some of them still are. But they have a couple of things in common; they love God, and they love people in a practical manner that requires them to give of themselves, and they now have some effective weapons to use gathered during their trip through hell. All in all, a magnificent fulfillment of Matthew 22:37-40.

The good news is that these folks are gathering together to form healing communities of varying sizes and descriptions; from a few folks who get together once a week to pray for the sick, to dozens who meet all over the city doing inner healing, deliverance, working with the abused, drug addicted, the abandoned, the sexually and relationally broken, the widows and the orphans, the prisons, half-way houses and shelters all across America and in foreign countries you'll never visit.

My wife and I have been extremely privileged these last few years to be able to travel and help establish some of them and then to nourish several others all across the southern US. It's fun to watch God do His thing and meet the special people who have answered His call.

What we have attempted to impart is a few of the tools God has taught us that will help an individual re-establish his/her personal identity. Somewhere in the process we can give them a few ideas that will allow God to assist them to recover lost and stolen dreams and visions for their lives, then given them some guidance in how to practically express it.

This is especially true for folks like artists and musicians. There is an old joke running around that asks the question, *"How can a musician (artist) end up with a million dollars? Answer: Start with two million."* What we have historically known is that this group of people are often referred to as "starving artists." The fact remains that if that's the driving force that God put in you, then there exists a means by which it can be satisfied and you can be fulfilled (and provided for) in the process. Yes, there is a training period and seasoning required to find your voice and your singular means of expression, along with sufficient skill, professionality and experience to carry it. Until you find it and then develop it, your peak earning years will still be ahead of you, but that doesn't mean that you will have to starve in the meantime. Remember, all the promises of provision detailed in Matthew 6 were written specifically for you.

Psalm 37:25 *"I have been young and I am now old, yet I have not seen the righteous abandoned, nor his children begging bread."*

See **www.the**worshipstudio.org

11

The Power and Importance of Purpose in walking in the spirit

Over the last few years I have had several detractors who vehemently came against what I am about to say because they still don't have a clue about what is God is up to in the earth and they have also very subtly been won over to the Americanized gospel of narcissism.

That viewpoint makes it all about us and tends to minimize God's overarching agenda in and for the earth, as well as for the balance of humanity. I would certainly be less than honest, and even in denial, if I said that what God was up to had absolutely nothing to do with you, because He has chosen to do everything through us, but His overall purpose has us positioned firmly in a supporting role, consequently, I can say without fear of His rebuke, "this really isn't about you."

Over the years much has been said and written in the Christian media about destiny and purpose and most of it has been pretty self-serving. By 'self-serving' I mean that all the peripheral messages of the church today are crafted to support the central theme and purpose of the institutional church, which tends to be wholly self serving. To be fair, most churches generally adhere to the centrality of Jesus crucified, risen and sitting at the right hand of the Father and that our only way to the Father is through His son Jesus the Christ. That is as it should be, but most of these religious clubs spend 85% of their resources providing a Sunday service so that you'll have a specific time to come and pay your club dues.

However, once you're in the club, the message changes. You now have to modify your behavior to properly represent the club and most of your free time and resources need to be spent supporting the services and activities of the club. So much for individualized purpose and destiny! You are now harnessed to a somewhat communistic organization that does not necessarily preach it, but certainly expects that the greater good of the club makes your purpose and destiny subservient to it. This ideology makes it clear that serving the institutional church is the highest good that man can aspire to, in fact, it is implied that it is the only Holy aspiration one could entertain, all else is carnal.

The reality of a Godly life is far from that viewpoint. Consider this. If everyone who works in a secular field were suddenly to become Holy and abandon their work in favor of pursuing sacred (institutional church) work, all of society would collapse within thirty days.

That dualistic viewpoint serves the church well, but is totally ungodly because it denies the fact that the vast majority of people were created by God to invent, manufacture and sell helpful products and services, some were created to repair things, some were created to beautify the things we see, use and inhabit, some were created for business, some for medicine, some for the military, some for engineering, even politics (God help us), on and on. This is who they are. They can't do anything else because that's how God intended them to live ... from the income provided by the product or service they provide; ie., the work of their hands. Consequently, there is no distinction made by God as to what is secular and what is sacred! It's all anointed because God created it that way!

This is so important for all of us to understand that I am going to repeat it; **there is no distinction made by God as to what is secular and what is sacred!** *(*So long as it's not illegal or immoral.)

So this means that you can legitimately expect to see anointed business men and women doing their thing all over town walking in the continuous blessing of the Lord on the lives and their businesses.

It is also important to understand this when your children are considering an occupation. A couple of years ago I was asked to join some other adults to do mock interviews for local High School seniors, where I asked each of them, "What do you want to do with your life?" Of the ten students four answered, "I'm going to college after I graduate." Not exactly a valid answer to the question. But I was stunned to find that seven of them had never been asked that question by a prominent adult in their lives. I have a tough time imagining that a parent could be so self-absorbed as to never have posed that question to their child. When I expressed it I was told that this was not the worst; I was told that this local High School actually had four students who were trying to finish school and were living in the woods because their home situations were so bad.

When you look down through history every great invention, every great novel, every great advancement in medicine, science, engineering, literature, statesmanship, art, music, entertainment, whatever, was accomplished at the hand of someone God put on this earth to pull that secret from heaven and see to it that it was made available to earth. That was their destiny, the fulfillment of their God ordained purpose.

Need a Biblical example?

Consider these two men of significance in the history of Israel; Saul and David. Both of these men came from markedly different backgrounds and upbringing. Saul was fairly well known; handsome, tall, well spoken and apparently well thought of enough that when the idea of a man being named king over Israel was being thrown around, his name came up quite naturally. David on the other hand was even forgotten by his own father when the prophet of the Lord was sent to him to anoint a king from among his sons.

Both men, while serving a King, sinned grievously, to the extent that the sin of each man was sufficient to have had them stoned to death. Both men realized the gravity of their sin and were obviously remorseful for it, and both men asked forgiveness for it. And yet, only one of them was declared by God Himself as, *"a man after my own heart."* (Acts 13:22)

So how do we reconcile that? Both committed major sin; one had his kingship ripped from his hands, the other got the kudos of God, *"a man after my own heart."* We know God killed a lot of people because of their sin, but that's not how he was relating to David.

The key is in the last part of that verse in,

> Acts 13:22, *"And when he had removed him (Saul), he raised up unto them David to be their king; to whom also he gave testimony, and said, I have found David the son of Jesse, a man after mine own heart, **which shall fulfill all my will**."*

In other words, the difference between the two men, David and Saul, was that only one of them had fulfilled his God-given purpose. That purpose was to do the will of God by leading Israel as King, under the leadership and direction of the Lord. Only David fulfilled his purpose, thereby gaining himself the high praise from God. You have to understand that sin destroys, we know that, but fulfillment of God ordained purposes trumps sin – and pretty much everything else - in God's eyes.

If you dare say that I'm condoning sin by that statement you weren't paying attention at all – go to the back of the class.

What I am saying is this …

> Luke 12:32 *"Fear not, little flock; for it is your Father's good pleasure to give you the **kingdom**."*
>
> Matthew 6:10 *"Thy **kingdom** come. Thy will be done in earth, as it is in heaven."*
>
> Matthew 6:33 *"But seek ye first the **kingdom of God**, and his righteousness; and all these things shall be added unto you."*
>
> Matthew10:7 *"And as ye go, preach, saying, The **kingdom of heaven** is at hand."*

These are all the words of Jesus and what he is emphasizing is that the **kingdom** is what it's all about. That is what the 1st

Adam was actually charged with (purpose) establishing; the rule of God on earth through man. He obviously failed. It is what Jesus (the 2nd Adam) came to permanently establish and charged us and His disciples to accomplish. If you are opposed to the establishment of His Kingdom, He's opposed to you! There is no other purpose.

If you will note, Jesus had the ultimate gift of discernment. He knew probably where every demon was and what they were doing within a 100 mile radius of Him at all times, and could have chosen to deal with every one of them harshly. However the only ones He dealt with were the ones who opposed Him directly, because He was on a mission to establish the Kingdom and no demon from hell was going to be allowed to stand in the way.

Knowing your purpose is mandatory.

The enemy (satan, the devil) knows that all too well, which is why he tries to thwart it in any way he can. Typically it is primarily through an all out assault on your identity. Since Jesus has already stripped satan of his weapons, the only thing he has at his disposal now is fear and deceit. He's learned to use both of them well and he's had centuries of practice.

There is a large article that somehow appeared as I began writing this section in the magazine Fast Company, Issue 190, November 2014, entitled *Find Your Mission, The Secrets of Generation Flux – How to Succeed in Business – and Life.* It is largely the results of interviewing a number of people from what the author defines as Generation Flux, those engaged in the post-2008 economy was still in a major state of flux. Those interviewed were CEO's, owners and Market leaders of companies large and small, and the topic is their philosophy of doing business in accord with an individual mission statement. A viable Mission Statement is a fundamental and traditional part of doing business in the public and private business sector. Actually engineering those statements to form a corporate culture and ideology to produce increased profits is nothing new for business, but we live in an age that deifies green and a reduced carbon footprint. This goes a step further.

The bottom line is that it is all about defining the mission so that the company stays on task in an effort to achieve the mission.

I quote for the article;

> "In this age of flux, people's sense of connection with their workplace has been declining. Last year (2013), Gallup came out with a detailed study of workers across US businesses. In all industries and all age groups, engagement was pitifully low. "The vast majority of US workers (70%) are not reaching their full potential," the report concluded. Yet in those pockets where passion for the job flourished, productivity, levels of customer service and profitability were all higher than average. "Companies with engaged work-forces have higher earnings per share," the report stated. Perhaps most important (and surprising) of all: "Engagement has a greater impact on performance than policies and perks.""

This understanding also covered employee contracts. The article went on to say,

> "A more effective contract meshes an individual's sense of purpose with that of the company. The Gallup report

notes that millennials, gen-Xers, and a baby boomers consider "mission and purpose" a valuable motivator."

It should be obvious that Biblical principles work, whether you are an Israeli King or a Captain of industry. A well thought out, firmly established and effectively communicated company mission statement is every bit as much a part of establishing the Kingdom of God as your local church's. Scripture tells us,

> *"And the LORD answered me, and said, Write the vision, and make it plain upon tables, that he may run that read it."* (Habakkuk 2:2)

So this begs the question, "Should I too have a personal mission statement?"

The answer is a resounding, "YES!!!!!!!"

Yes, yes, YES!!! If you don't know where you're going, any road will take you there. The problem is, most of the places it takes you … you'll hate.

That was my problem. I exited High School with the words of President John F. Kennedy ringing in my ears. A couple of years earlier we had lost the race to get into space to the Russians and we needed a major technological boost to catch up. He made an appeal for more mathematicians, chemists, engineers and scientists to join the race so we could rapidly close the gap. I chose electrical engineering, primarily because I thought my dad would like that, and he was an engineer of sorts. When LBJ assumed the Presidency following the assassination of JFK, I should have reviewed my options.

Upon exiting college I was hired by an engineering consulting house in Houston, Texas. I rapidly found out that I hated design engineering.

But what's a fellow to do? I had too much invested to quit and no clue what I'd do if I did. So I persevered for three and a half years and then moved into technical sales. Again, I could do it and was reasonably successful at it, but it didn't really ring my bell. In spite of it I climbed the corporate ladder and served as Director of Sale and Marketing for two industrial manufacturers. What was missing all along was an understanding of my purpose. I didn't really realize the fullness of it until some years later when I began managing a high-end 100 bed assisted living facility on the north side of Atlanta, GA, which brought the entire scope of it into focus for me; the perfect blend of business and a pastoral role, caring for people physically, emotionally and spiritually.

This whole subject harkens back to my statement in the Introduction, what we have come to realize over the course of ministering to people for 30-plus years is that the real goal of healing our wounds, dealing with the generational curses, breaking the habits of sin and patterns of iniquity in our lives is the discovery, re-discovery, or perhaps the un-covering of an individual's identity, which is a prerequisite to the discovery of personal purpose.

When we come to realize who we are, we can then begin to see why we're here (our eyes are open to what we need to see in light of who we really are) and that enables us to pursue it. The pursuit of it brings fulfillment and self satisfaction, which is the realization of the words of Jesus when He said, "*I am come that you might have **life and life abundant**.*" As a bonus when you fulfill your purpose, the Kingdom of God is established, demonstrated and advanced. It all works together.

So what does all this have to so with walking in the spirit? Neither your spirit, nor your flesh can prosper in something you were not created to do. Yes, you can walk in shoes that are either too large or two small for you, but your feet and your emotional attitude will suffer for it. And it you stay in them long enough your walk and eventually the rest of your life, becomes conformed to the limitation of your feet.

My decision to enter heady field of electrical engineering was formulated as a result of a purely intellectual exercise of trying to figure out what I wanted to do, squirrel! Had I been in touch with my human spirit, where my true identity lay ripe for discovery, I believe that the story of the last 53 years would have been a much more interesting and productive story. Why? There is absolutely no comparison between what I am doing for a living now and what I was doing then. It's like night and day. And the life I get to live now is much preferable to one I struggled to live back then.

12

Evidence of Kingdom Responsibility

This Chapter should perhaps have been better titled as one of the ways to show that you are discharging your Kingdom responsibilities. But that would be a bit too long. Although that may well be an apt description of what I want to talk about next, there is an aspect of it that is strictly a benefit ... if you choose to engage it as being the sole purpose of the exercise.

God created us to work from a position of rest ... from a place devoid of striving. That is best achieved when we are rested physically, mentally and spiritually and in order to accommodate it we have to have an environment in our home, and hopefully in our businesses, that is conducive to rest, relaxation and rejuvenation. When our homes or business environments are not peaceful it wears on us quickly. We become short with those around us, the atmosphere around us is filled with noise, clutter and clatter that makes it difficult to think clearly and consistently make good decisions. That wears on us physically and in time our health becomes affected. Poor rest and bad health impair us spiritually.

You and I have a choice to establish the atmosphere in our home and business. Often we just assume that whatever it is, so long as it's not too bothersome, it is what it and it will always be that way and I'll get used to it. So we do nothing. If that's your current normal thought process, I've got some news for you. It doesn't have to be that way.

There are several things you have to understand. First among them is the fact that according to Genesis 1, you and I were the only things God chose to make out of the earth. (We do get a little more information on this topic in Genesis 2.) Everything else He spoke into existence. That declares to me that we have a special relationship with the earth. One that is somewhat symbiotic. With that said, let me make it perfectly clear that the earth is NOT your mother, as some would assert.

Secondly, He put us (humans) at the top of the food chain and declared that we had to take care of the rest of this creation for it would provide our daily sustenance. See Genesis 1:26 and 29-30.

Then He gave some further instruction in Genesis 1:28,

> *"Be fruitful, and multiply, and replenish the earth, and subdue it: and have dominion over ... and over every living thing that moveth upon the earth."* (KJV)

Let me break it down a little further for emphasis ...

> *Be fruitful,*
>
> *and multiply,*
>
> *and replenish the earth,*
>
> *and subdue it:*
>
> *and have dominion*

We certainly get the idea that Adam and Eve where to have a bunch of kids so that items one, two and three could be checked off. But what of items four and five? What needed to be subdued and needed dominion exercised over it? I certainly don't think it was either crab grass or cudzu, for satan had yet to get around to perverting those plant varieties yet.

It is my guess that what needed to be subdued and what needed to be held in subjection was the rebellion that was in the earth brought here when Lucifer was thrown down out of heaven to earth. In other words, God had given the earth into the hands of men (Psalms 115:16) and at this point Lucifer (satan) was simply an unemployed vagrant wandering around trashing as much of God's original creation as he could. Hence, man's assignment to sort it all out.

Well, you know the next chapter of this history. Adam and Eve blew it and essentially satan, who had previously only been a potential menace, was now an official menace with considerable influence. But that transaction didn't nullify the initial charge of God to man one iota with regards to our responsibility to care for the earth. It was, and still is intact. You and I still have the same responsibility. However, since you and I would probably be no more successful than Adam and Eve were in the subduing/dominion department without some help, God had to send in some help in the form of Jesus, whose spirit now dwells within us.

I repeat: God's initial charge for humans has not been canceled. It is still in effect.

In the several thousand years since then, man has listened more to satan than to God and has made a pretty big mess of things. Among those early inhabitants were the sons of Adam and Eve;

Cain and Able. Cain was a farmer and Able was a rancher. Cain got mad at Able because God accepted Able's sacrifice and not his, so his logic said he needed to get rid of his brother, so he killed him. (An early form of current day political strategy.) In response, God pronounced a curse on Cain for what he had done.

Here's what God said to Cain,

> *Genesis 4:10-12 "And the LORD said, "What have you done? The voice of your brother's blood is crying to me from the ground.*
> *11 And now <u>you are cursed from the ground</u>, which has opened its mouth to receive your brother's blood from your hand.*
> *12 When you work the ground, <u>it shall no longer yield to you its strength</u>. You shall be a fugitive and a wanderer on the earth." (ESV)*

Now there are a couple of things that need to be pointed out here. First of all we understand that all sin defiles. It defiles the person who sins, it defiles the one sinned against, and it defiles the ground upon which it was committed. The price of the defilement of the land is often times no longer paid solely by the one who committed the act of defilement, but the ones who inhabit the land hundreds, if not thousands of years after the original defilement because of what is said in verses 11 and 12.

From these verses we see that It was actually not God that pronounced the curse, but the land itself. God only articulated it as though He were the mediator between Man and the earth.

The ground essentially said, I've had it with you! I am no longer going to yield my strength to you. We can also read that word "strength" as; capacity, capability, vigor, force, might, ability. I know you are thinking, "Wait just a minute! The EARTH did what?"

Consider this:

Abraham is told by God in Genesis 12:1 to pack up and leave Southern Syria (Haran) and head for the Promised Land, which the Lord will show him and give it to him and his ancestor forever. Now verse five tells us that Abram is once rich dude: he's got lots of camels, servants, cattle, horses, sheep and Lord knows what else, but he's got lots f it.

> The Lord didn't tell him how to get there.
>
> The Lord didn't give him a map.
>
> The Lord didn't give him an angel to guide him.
>
> The Lord didn't give him a pillar of fire to follow at night.
>
> The Lord didn't give him a cloud to follow by day.
>
> And GPS hadn't been invented yet.

So how does a man with hundreds of animals negotiate a Southern journey of 400 miles without directions, a guide or a map? He is forced to follow the provision of grass for his flocks and herds and water for them, himself, and his family. How does he make that happen?

Is it possible that the land itself guided he and his herds and flocks almost 400 miles south by providing everything he needed, exactly where he needed it? In other words, providing its strength (capabilities) to him." I think that is precisely what happened.

Here's another semi-random thought I've had that deserves some consideration. How many times have you pulled into a crowded parking lot looking for a place to park and a spot opened up right up front for you? We have casually written if off to chance or pure coincidence and nothing more, but what if it was the land itself that recognized you and guided you to the open (or soon to be open) spot as soon as you pulled onto the property?

Here's another point to remember when considering this topic; you and I are the only thing that God chose to make out of the earth itself. Everything else the Lord spoke into existence. So you and I were not only hand crafted by God, but in crafting us he did it in a manner such that we were better suited to have a special relationship with the earth. Having been made from the earth, we have been given responsibility for it and stewardship over it, and one day our bodies will return to the dust of it when we croak.

So what does that mean for us in the 21st Century? Scripture tells us that *"we've been given everything we need for daily life and Godliness."* (2Peter 1:3) If the promise was true for those who lived exclusively in an agrarian society, then it is also true for those of us living in a mechanized and digitally driven society. The strength we need in this day and age is also a form of provision, as it was for Abram, however, in our society it takes the form of revelation, ideas, understanding, wisdom and favor.

> *Deuteronomy 8:18 "You shall remember the LORD your God, for it is he who gives you power to get wealth, that*

> *he may confirm his covenant that he swore to your fathers, as it is this day."*

I believe that it is apparent from what we have already read that the land cooperated expressly with the will of God to produce life, health and peace in the life of a believer so that God may confirm His covenant with us, ratified in the blood of Jesus Christ. This includes giving us the revelation, ideas, understanding, wisdom and favor required to make wealth.

To make sure that the blessings we are given are passed on to the balance of mankind, He put a couple of other principles in motion that would insure that the ripples of His blessings would extended to the limits of society. Here are a couple of them;

In 1726, Isaac Newton shared the apple anecdote with William Stukeley, who included it in a biography, "Memoirs of Sir Isaac Newton's Life," published in 1752. According to Stukeley, *"After dinner, the weather being warm, we went into the garden, & drank tea under the shade of some apple trees... he told me, he was just in the same situation, as when formerly, the notion of gravitation came into his mind.... occasion'd by the fall of an apple, as he sat in a contemplative mood."*

In 1907 Albert Einstein realized that his Special theory of Relativity was not complete. The principle of relativity was only applicable to observers moving with a constant velocity. It also did not fit with the Newtonian description of gravity.

Einstein, being a patent officer, did not have access to laboratory equipment. To compensate, he had to engage himself in thought experiments. He considered various scenarios in his head and worked through them all step by step, which he often did either outdoors under a tree in a nearby park, or while on his small boat while sailing.

(Here's a useless aside: Although Einstein was an avid sailor, one biographer declares that he was quite poor at it, often becoming seemingly becalmed even when there was an available breeze sufficient to propel him.)

As a sailor, I have to say (somewhat disappointedly) that I have never experienced such an epiphany while sailing, perhaps because I am a better sailor, however, I am much more prone to it while fly fishing for trout. (Not sure what that says about my fishing prowess.)

The only way that the land is rendered 'unable' or is prevented from yielding its strength to us is either by our own sin and unwillingness to follow the leadings of the Lord (shutting down our heart and ears to Him) …. or … the intentional defilement of the land by the human agents that the enemy used to defile it.

All this to say … your home should be a sanctuary, regardless of the circumstances of life. It should provide you with an environment that is conducive to rest, restoration and rejuvenation of your body and soul, while allowing you to clearly hear the Lord and receive what you need from Him. But in order to make it such you are going to have to deal either with the residual defilement in or on the structure, or in the land that the structure occupies, or both. I call that act, land cleansing.

13

The Body as a Prophetic Telegraph

The use of the word "telegraph" is intentional. Though in our technology driven world it is archaic, I prefer to see it as simplistic. One individual communicated to another through a series of dots and dashes. It took time to communicate in such a fashion and seemed arduous enough that it spawned a drive to find other means. It was, however, quite sufficient for the time. Another observation is that the message came in slowly, letter by letter, word by word, and this is somewhat similar to the way Holy Spirit speaks to us. He seldom blasts us with the entire message simultaneously but gives it to us line upon line, precept upon precept, here a little, there a little.

Over the years of praying for people with physical issues, I have always sought for a way to be more effective, desiring to see more healed as a result. Actually, I think this is a natural consequence of praying for someone and not experiencing results we desire, or only seeing minimal results. So I pressed into the Lord. What resulted was interesting from several perspectives.

First, English is not necessarily Holy Spirit's first language; he certainly uses it, but He also resorts (at least with me) to several other means of communication. Why is that? It is because communication is always about relationship. The opportunity to pray for someone is always an invitation to a conversation for the purpose of enhancing the relationship, both for you and the one receiving prayer. So over the years Holy Spirit taught me several "languages" if you will. I am still building vocabulary in many areas, and this is one of those.

Second, the verse that declares that we are "fearfully and wonderfully made" (Psalms 139:14) could easily have been four or five chapters. We are such incredibly complex creatures it's astonishing! We can parse our beings into several portions, such as "spirit, soul and body" (1 Thessalonians 5:23) for the sake of definition and discussion. The interconnectivity between and among these elements, however, is not only inseparable, but vital.

What we have found through operating healing rooms and praying for people for the last dozen years or so, is that about 85% of the things people suffer with physically are rooted in emotional and/or spiritual issues. You can pray against the fruit and see some success, but the final solution obviously lies in cutting the root. There had to be a way for Holy Spirit to unveil the root in a much shorter period of time (i.e., during a prayer session) so that the root could be effectively severed.

One of the ways Holy Spirit began to direct me was through the pain or malady of the individual receiving prayer. Check out the material called *"The Body as a Prophetic Telegraph"* on our web site at www.jimandpatbanks.com/resources. It will help you learn how to look for the roots of pain in an individual's body by giving you insight into the source of the symptoms – if the Holy Spirit doesn't tell you what it is right out of the gate.

One of the other ways that Holy Spirit has chosen to talk to me is through pains in my own body which relate specifically to the issues of the one receiving prayer. Understand that these are not 'sympathetic' pains that might be a function of compassion, but a specific form of communication from Holy Spirit given to point to the root issue. If the pains happen to be in the same place as the one you are praying for, you would refer to that as a Word of Knowledge. However, if the person you are praying for is struggling with some relational issue, the pain is targeting a specific source, which is why learning the vocabulary of this language is important.

Whenever I experience a pain in the middle of a ministry session, I usually know that Holy Spirit is trying to tell me something. The interesting thing about this is that the pain will not go away until I have led them through addressing it. That could simply be a prayer or another form of ministry. If an opportunity does not arise to deal with it, I will continue to experience the pain until they drive away and off the property. Such is Holy Spirit's desire to resolve issues.

Rather than lay a few of the ways God uses to speak to us for you I would suggest that you go to Kathie Walter's web site http://www.goodnews.netministries.org/goodnews.html for a couple of them. From the Home Page go to Kathie Walters/ebooks/ and buy two items; *The Seers List* and *Health Related Mind Sets*. Between these two items the Lord will give you a basis for education in how to minister to the needs of others through the Holy Spirit language He wants to build with you.

Understand that what Holy Spirit builds with you may or may not look anything like what Kathie Walters has been able to establish. Mine is similar in many respects but differs in many areas and is certainly not as extensive. It's about the opportunity to enter into a conversation with Holy Spirit, not the end result.

Another way to interpret pain.

There have been occasions when in the course of ministering to someone Holy Spirit will make it very plain that the individual's issue is due to the presence of a demon. When you begin to address it, obviously the individual must repent for whatever sin gave it the legal right to enter and renounce the permission they have given that has allowed it to stay. Because demons are legalists, accuracy in naming each of those things is very important. You can't just fire in the general direction and hope to hit something, otherwise you will likely cause it to go into hiding and extend the whole process significantly.

When I get to the point of taking authority over the demon in the name of Jesus, it is helpful to know where the blasted thing is so you will know when it's gone. On many occasions, as often noted in the Bible, the demon will try to trash the host in anger before it leaves, thus there may be pain, choking, writhing, etc. Obviously when the display ends, you know the deed is done. But when dealing with a spirit of self-hate, which is quite often as is the case with many of the people I work with, that particular demon doesn't put up such resistance, not that it goes without so much as a whimper. Consequently, it is helpful to know when it's gone.

When dealing with it in someone I have been ministering to I usually begin to feel its presence somewhere around the pyloric valve above my stomach. I usually feel it as a golf ball sized ball of something similar to indigestion which slowly rises up my esophagus and up and out through my throat. When the deliverance is complete both of us always feel a lot better.

The reason I mention this is because the way God created us was spirit, soul and body, all working together with the spirit calling the shots. And the order of the list was how we were designed to live – it's the divine order and still is. If you have established your brain as the leader of the band instead of your spirit, then it wants to control everything, but tends to leave your spirit and your body out of the mix. That means, if the situation you are facing requires some supernatural input, you are going to be seriously outta luck solving the problem. If your situation requires big time help and you are the only resource you can lean on then you are in for a rough road. You have to begin living by the spirit.

One last example;

To live as a Christian in the Asheville, NC area is to be daily acquainted with the effects of living in an environment that is heavily tainted with occult practices because those that practice it carry so much open animosity toward God and His church.

Consequently, they are frequently, praying against your health, your marriage, your family dynamics, your finances and your business and your church. This is a constant assignment against every pastor and every ministry. This doesn't include all the sacrifices made at the time of each new moon and the Winter & Summer Solstices. It is one of the reasons why doing church in that valley is so difficult, and frankly it's a non-stop pain in the butt to have to deal with. The name of Jesus can easily kill a bunch of the junk they stir up, so the damage isn't permanent. My guess is that you really have to be mentally deficient to have to keep throwing dust into the wind when there are so many fun things you could be doing.

I always feel the witchcraft prayers on the back of my neck, similar to the manner in which we collectively experience the effects of stress. If I do not deal with it immediately it will build until it also involves my shoulders as well. It is easy to break off in the name of Jesus, if you understand that it is there, but so many people think it's simply from the stress they are under and put up with it. That way they give in to one of the greatest weapons of the enemy, "to wear out the saints."

So pay attention to what your body is telling you.

14

One More Thing ...

In our efforts to operate by the spirit we have to be cautious that we are actually adhering to the principle foundational pillars of the Kingdom: love and relationship. Anything done outside of that is accomplished out of our own selfish ambition or some baser fleshly (or even cultural) perception of what is right and wrong. That will always get us into trouble.

We are familiar with ministries founded and operated by people whom the Lord chose for that purpose, but who have strayed from the purity of their heart that established the ministry. As a result these ministries have largely become guided by rules, mottoes and slogans (and the need for funding) rather than the heart that Jesus gave them.

We are not always in touch with the motivations of our heart, in spite of being totally convinced that we are. A number of years ago our oldest son was preparing to be married and I thought that it would be a great opportunity to take the whole family for ministry down to South Carolina at Jack Frost's Ministry. We could stay at the beach and I would get to play golf with one or both of the boys while somebody got ministry and Pat could get all the sun she wanted. When it came time for my turn I was surprised by the outcome. During the session the gentleman who was ministering to me asked, "Why do you do what you do?" At the time, I thought to myself, "This has got to be a trick question. I pray for people, what more noble enterprise could one possibly aspire to?" He interrupted my silence with, "There is this interesting little verse in Proverbs that says, "There is profit in all labor." It is the foundation of charity. If we didn't feel good about ourselves when we did something good for others, there would be no such thing as charity. So I ask you again …. Why do you do what you do?"

I had no idea that my supposed totally selfless act was indeed polluted by such selfishness.

In Psalm 139:23-24, David said,

> "Search me, O God, and know my heart: try me, and know my thoughts:
> 24 And see if there be any wicked way in me, and lead me in the way everlasting."

Our problem, that David was probably aware of in his own life, is that we are not always aware of the hidden motivations of our own hearts, and I can do nothing about them until I can see them. You can't do anything with, or about, the things you do not know.

Normally we look at the negative side of all things Because that's what our Western culture requires us to do; correct your mistakes, heal the brokenness, improve your weaknesses, all so that you can avoid failure. But why are we not also dedicated to searching out our strengths, our gifting and unique abilities that our wounds have attempted to keep us blind to? There are many amazing things He has put in us that we are so far also unaware of?

15

Some Thoughts on Spiritual Gifts

It is understood that a book that gives you some specific encouragement in walking (or stumbling) by the Spirit, better have something to say about what we have come to refer to as spiritual gifts. These are referenced in Romans 12 and other scriptures,

> *Romans 12:4-8 "For as in one body we have many members, and the members do not all have the same function,*
> *5 so we, though many, are one body in Christ, and individually members one of another.*
> *6 Having gifts that differ according to the grace given to us, let us use them: if **prophecy**, in proportion to our faith;*
> *7 if **service**, in our serving; the one who **teaches**, in his teaching;*
> *8 the one who **exhorts**, in his exhortation; the one who **contributes**, in generosity; the one who **leads**, with zeal; the one who does **acts of mercy**, with cheerfulness." (ESV)*

> *Romans 1:11-12 "For I long to see you, that I may impart to you some spiritual gift to strengthen you—*

> 12 that is, that we may be mutually encouraged by each other's faith, both yours and mine.
>
> 2Corinthians 12:12 Truly the signs of an apostle were wrought among you in all patience, in **signs**, and **wonders**, and **mighty deeds**."
>
> Ephesians 4:11 "And he gave the **apostles**, the **prophets**, the **evangelists**, the **shepherds** and **teachers**,
> 12 to equip the saints for the work of ministry, for building up the body of Christ,
> 13 until we all attain to the unity of the faith and of the knowledge of the Son of God, to mature manhood, to the measure of the stature of the fullness of Christ,"

Obviously, as we are living our daily work-a-day lives, we are privileged to be able to connect with a large variety of people who have no relationship with God, and the further our culture slips into secularism the greater that population will be. All the people we connect with are our sphere of influence, ie, people that we can impact in some way. Since we are vitally connected to Holy Spirit we have access to some 'inside' information about them and their futures.

Just as people are not jealous of poverty, they are also not drawn to people who are self-absorbed. They are drawn to those who love openly and understand that they are connected to a higher power that can impact their needs. Prophesy does that quite easily, as does healing, along with "**signs, and wonders, and mighty deeds**."

There are plenty of books out there that are more effective in conveying what these gifts are and how they look operating through various individuals, so rather than trying to reinvent the wheel, I am going to defer to them to educate them. You just need to understand that each of us has access to them and we were created to operate in them for the benefit of those around us.

However everything has to operate through love ..

> Romans 12:9-10 "Let love be genuine. Abhor what is evil; hold fast to what is good.
> 10 Love one another with brotherly affection. Outdo one another in showing honor."

End

Made in the USA
Coppell, TX
13 November 2020